An
EXCEPTIONAL
ROMANCE

***Igniting** the marriage of your dreams
by replacing routine with **passion***

KATE AND STEVE DAHLIN

"I have had the joyous pleasure of knowing Kate and Steve since they started dating. It has been a privilege watching them work together as a true team to prioritize, share, and celebrate as a married couple. Together, they have intentionally invested in their marriage and are now sharing their experiences and life lessons with other young couples. God's Word is the foundation of their marriage, and sharing their experiences is their calling. I know that couples of all ages will appreciate their openness, practical insights, and wit. Enjoy!"

—Jim Bowes
Former president and CEO of Peach State Integrated Technologies, Inc.

"In this case, you can judge a book by the cover. The Dahlins have blended their experience, hope, and passion into timeless principles this generation can get excited about and actually apply in the real world."

—Ted Lowe
CEO of MarriedPeople.org

"Kate and Steve have walked with us through our dating, engagement, and early married season. They are a continual encouragement in our pursuit of Jesus and each other by exemplifying a marriage that is ignited by adventure, passion, and love. The stories and wisdom in this book come from their journey and will have an eternal impact on your marriage, as it has on ours."

—Megan and Jared Fulks

CONTENTS

INTRODUCTION

Kate and Steve

We are attracted to another person at a soul level not
because that person is our unique complement, but because
by being with that individual, we are somehow provided
with an impetus to become whole ourselves.

—Edgar Cayce

Have you ever heard of the one-degree principle? It refers to reaching a destination. For example, for every degree you fly off course, you will miss your desired destination by ninety-two feet for every mile flown. So if you were flying from JFK to LAX and were off by one degree, you would be over fifty miles off course.

Wanting a good marriage is not enough. Small course adjustments can significantly impact your romance through the years, but you have to determine your direction. Your ultimate trajectory depends on it. So where are you heading right now?

It was just a few years into our marriage when we sat down with some dear friends on a vacation and discussed the topic of blending two unique lives into one. Out of all the words our friends could have used to describe this process, they chose *hard*. We were stunned.

These friends had been married for less than a year. *It's hard ...*

already? we thought. We had some deep conversations about the perceived struggles of marriage. After all, we too were at the starting gate, and culture paints a pretty dismal outlook of marriage through marketing, movies, and sitcoms. It launched us into a decade of seeking answers and strategies for creating the best marriage possible.

That vacation left us with a determined purpose to help others (as well as ourselves) in this journey. In just a few short years, we passionately entered into a ministry of mentoring couples around their desired growth areas and relational dreams. We were zealous in proclaiming the how-tos and do-nots in order to equip young hearts for the foreverness of marriage.

But here is the thing—it doesn't have to be hard. In those early years (and even today), many friends and strangers said that the honeymoon phase would eventually end, and the rose-colored glasses would fade. People said that our feet weren't on the ground and that we were blinded by love. And another common phrase: "Just wait; it'll hit you."

How anyone can be that negative and pessimistic about the institution and covenant of marriage is completely beyond us. We believe it can be fireworks, connection, joy, and one of the few constants in this variable world.

The daily choices you make are crucial to maintaining a vigorous relationship throughout the course of your life together. The ideas presented in this book are preventatives. The outcome is fun and exhilarating and will be supported and sustained by healthy habits. We want the intricacies of your relationship to be automatic, easy, and incredibly life-giving.

When you sign up for married life, you don't go into it with a negative mind-set. You are over the moon in love. You expect to beat the odds; you are the exception to the norm. The chemistry and nuances of your relationship are one of a kind. Plus, you have God on your side, and he created all of these relationships. There is nothing left to do but make the leap together.

If you wanted a book about working on your marriage, you chose the wrong one (all the men should cheer here). Romance is not work when you get it right. It's inspiring and magnetic, and everybody will want to know your secret.

There is a concept in business called *linked prosperity*, which we strongly support. It basically means that if we thrive, you also should thrive. This is why we share our story. We are still wearing those rose-colored glasses when it comes to each other. We are best friends and each other's favorite person. We love doing life together. We always say to each other, "You make me the best version of myself." And we deeply want that for your relationship too.

We are not experts by any means. We have written this book because we are also in the middle of married life and are wanting to see everyone experience growth in their relationship. We challenge you to continually cultivate the fire that started your romance and fuel it to the next level and beyond. We pray that these pages will inspire you to allow the sparks to fly.

Tuesday, May 19, 2009

Happy Two-Year Anniversary

My dearest Kate,

First of all, I want you to know how much I love you. My admiration and appreciation of you grows each and every day. It is amazing to see how fast two years have gone by, and I am yet again reminded of how lucky I am to have met you in Panama City Beach. The Lord works in mysterious ways, and I often reflect on the uniqueness in which we were brought together in the summer of 2005.

Normally at this time, I would be buying you a dozen freshly cut roses and adding a Hallmark card to go with it. However, due to the plethora of bouquets currently in our humble abode from recital weekend, I decided to throw tradition out the window and be creative in expressing my love to you this year. So I will give it a try.

There is a passage in scripture that I often quote or reference, and it is because it holds a special place in my heart. On Saturday morning, May 19, 2007, Ben and I were having Bible time and praying in the hotel courtyard. We were reading on marriage and our study led us to the following text in Proverbs 18:22: "He who finds a wife finds a good thing, and obtains favor from the LORD." That morning, I was hit with the realization that I had found not only my wife and soul mate but a beautiful, caring, compassionate, sensitive, respectful, pure, and God-fearing woman. And because I had found you, I had obtained favor from my heavenly Father.

Saying "I do" was the easy part. I've been waiting my whole life to say those two words to you. Even so, living up to the public vows I took on our wedding day and exercising flawlessly what scripture commands in regard how one treats and honors one's wife—every day of every week and every month of these two years—has been a challenge, nonetheless. While I cannot guarantee that I will never let you down, I can promise you the following:

With every fiber in my being and every breath that I take, I will love and cherish you with all of my heart and will purpose to prefer your needs above mine, treat you with the utmost respect, and honor you as long as I live. Happy anniversary, angel.

Always and forever yours,
Stephen

Life is a mess, with all of its twists and turns, but your marriage does not have to be messy. Your romance can be the best experience this side of heaven. We are now in our second decade of marriage and are a living testament to this. You may not think so, but you can have something magical. For any couple in a relationship today, we believe that the most opportunity and the greatest gain for love is now. It is not a lost art; commitment is not gone; and hope has not vanished.

John 10:10 says that Jesus came so that you may have life and have it abundantly. This is our prayer for you. Let us shift our outlook and direction so that we may stay out of the marriage self-help aisles and cultivate the best life from the onset. We ask you to join us on this wild and gorgeous life as a couple! Seize it. This book is written and dedicated to you—to everyone who wants to see God's plan for marriage and wants to create an exceptional romance.

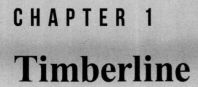

CHAPTER 1

Timberline

—Steve

People rarely succeed unless they have fun in what they are doing.

—Dale Carnegie

It's amazing that people believe they have to sacrifice the things they enjoy doing or that make them happy once they get married. Most sitcoms today equate marriage to the death of everything fun. Have you entertained this notion?

I came across a billboard on my way to the office the other day from a furniture company that is only open Friday through Sunday: "Let us satisfy your wife three days out of the week. Can you?"

Our culture is constantly downplaying marriage romance, and the jokes seem to be endless about lack of sex and boredom. Movies and TV portray couples as roommates with separate lives, careers, and hobbies.

Personal hobbies are great things. I enjoy exercising, drawing/painting, grilling, playing the drums, and doing anything on the water, as well as golfing, golfing, and more golfing! These talents and enjoyments are the unique thumbprints of God's design on my life. To ignore or suppress them would be like picking a beautiful bouquet of flowers and then putting them in a vase without water. Excessively focusing on your hobbies would be like overwatering a plant. Both eventually cause death and rob you of the flowers' beauty.

Freedom is a result of trust. Kate has known from the beginning, with certainty, that none of my hobbies would ever come before her or our future family. She had to trust me, but I also have upheld that trust. Most of us know which hobby seems to be the predominant hot button, which indicates a lack of balance. Get this order right, and you both will be in a happier state.

But what do you enjoy doing *together*? What steps have you taken to foster togetherness in your relationship? What experiences are you sharing, and what new hobbies are you exploring and developing that you can do as a team?

On one occasion, the wife of a young couple that we mentor was articulating her new husband's love of hunting and fishing. She was more of a shopper and an around-the-town kind of girl. Not a big deal—opposites sometimes attract—but if they stopped there, then life would become progressively more difficult. This isn't a recipe for success, because separate hobbies will always leave you separate.

When was the last time you truly got away with your spouse? Let me be clear—I'm not talking about heading out for a weekend trip (although those quick getaways are sometimes just what the doctor ordered). I'm talking about the following:

- having phone silence
- abstaining from email
- abstaining from chores
- relishing late breakfasts over mimosas
- taking long, quiet walks
- reading a good book
- doing a unique family activity
- getting lost gazing into a fire

- spending time in a hot tub
- cooking a multicourse meal
- stargazing late at night (for us, once the kids are asleep!)
- cuddling under a blanket with the person of your dreams
- watching the sunrise or sunset
- swinging in a hammock
- hiking or getting on the water

My family has a place in the Colorado mountains. It's simple, but the views are gorgeous. My grandparents picked the land back in the late seventies and built the house themselves, and it's been in the family ever since. I have fond memories from my childhood of lying on an orange shag carpet, throwing rocks in the lake, hiking, camping, and learning to ski on the slopes of Arapahoe Basin and Keystone.

Early in our marriage, Kate and I took a trip together to hike, explore, and enjoy God's country. There is a small, special book at the mountain house that highlights various trails in the area, and we've all made notes on the hikes we've taken through the years and commented on ease of access, trail length, scenery, and whether the view was worth the climb.

Kate and I had chosen a path and set out early one morning for the trailhead. Several trail choices were presented to us, everything from beginner to expert. We picked a moderate hike, and over the next few hours, we welcomed the cool morning breeze, the sound of leaves rustling in the wind, myriad birds singing, and the sound of water trickling and babbling through unseen streams. We were having so much fun together that we unknowingly missed our turn at a fork in the trail and veered off on an unmarked path. The topology shifted quickly, and we began a rapid ascent up the mountain face. It was constant stop and go, and we paused multiple times to catch our breath, shed layers of clothing due to the heat, and pull out rain gear as an afternoon storm rolled through the mountains.

While packing our suitcases, Kate had made multiple comments about the number of clothing items and layers we were taking. There was no doubt in her mind that I was overplanning and overthinking this aspect of our trip. I, however, had done this before, while she had only been to Colorado during the ski season. I tried to explain the somewhat unpredictable nature of the weather and how quickly things could change. But she couldn't fully believe me until she experienced it for herself. For example, it could be eighty degrees, with a bright-blue sky and no humidity, and within the hour, it could drop thirty-plus degrees, and there could be rain, sleet, and snow (depending on your elevation). Then it might return to sunny and eighty degrees, as if nothing had happened. My dad has an amazing story of how it snowed in June while he was playing tennis with some college friends.

In marriage, you will weather these drastic and sometimes unforeseeable fluctuations in life. Weather patterns change, sometimes at a moment's notice. Jobs could be lost. Sickness or a doctor's diagnosis could make life seemingly stand still. Issues with immediate family, car challenges, legal battles, infertility, and many other problems can happen suddenly. How will you react? What will help you weather these storms? We believe managing our marriage is like our hiking trip; doing so requires the proper equipment, and it starts with the Lord and each other, along with a little grit, determination, perseverance, and faith.

Wildflowers peppered the trail with brilliant natural colors, and the smell of pine and aspen encompassed us. Our calves were burning, and our breathing was heavy, but eventually we could see the timberline. Now that the view was no longer obstructed, it was simply incredible. We pulled out our jackets and hats to combat the chilling winds as we completed our climb to the peak. Energy, excitement, and adrenaline coursed through our bodies.

We stood on the east ridge of Keller Mountain, hugging, laughing, and looking in awe at the beauty surrounding us. You can see a lot from ten thousand feet! We had covered over nine miles of trail and a change of fourteen hundred feet in elevation in about eight hours. And we did it together, pushing each other on, laughing, singing, joking, telling stories, sometimes being quiet, and enjoying each other's company along the way. You have to take this same approach to your daily life and romance.

Men, how are you energizing your dating life? I'll be honest; unless we push ourselves and fuel our creative ideas, most of us will just go into autopilot once the ring is on her finger, and we say, "I do." But this is only the start, my friends. You have a lifetime to unravel the mysteries of her heart, personality, and desires. There are no shortcuts here. I guarantee you the view will be worth the climb.

And you don't need a lot of money to go on a date. If that's your excuse, let's get it off the table right now. *The date is about the pursuit, not the event.* Sure, we've ridden in a limo around downtown Atlanta, done a helicopter tour, sat in box seats in the Falcons' stadium, and had five-course meals at some of the best restaurants. But those experiences came much later for us.

Even now, sometimes the simplest of plans can yield the greatest returns in romance—things like reading, doing home projects, playing board games, or stargazing. Take the mattress off your bed, put it in front of the TV, make popcorn, and have a movie-marathon night. One of our favorite things to do in the evening is to sit on our front steps, shoulder to shoulder, and talk. So what habits will you change in order to energize your dating life, starting today?

I had lost sight of this truth early in our marriage. I was a Scrooge with our money and felt like there was no need to go out when we could hang out all the time at the apartment. A few years into our marriage, a wise mentor of mine asked a question over coffee that rocked my world:

"How much money does it cost to maintain your car every year, including insurance, payments, gas, and maintenance?"

I took a few moments to add the figures in my head. I was driving an old Chevy Blazer at the time, and it seemed to always need maintenance. I gave him my answer, thinking little of it.

He then asked, "How much money are you spending on dating your wife?"

I had no words and was completely embarrassed because the stack ranking wasn't even close. In that moment, I was confronted with the immaturity and failure of my choices as a man and a husband and didn't like what I saw. This current trajectory would not take me to the destination I had in mind. I had to make a change and do it quickly. That was the turning point for me, and our dating life has been exceptional ever since. Today, we schedule our babysitters in advance and make dating as predictable in our monthly schedule and budget as a haircut or a family meal. I'll go without Starbucks coffee, cable TV, golf, and other extras (if I have to) in order to keep our dates alive. It's nonnegotiable, in my opinion.

It is impossible to foresee what curve balls life will throw at you. We've gone through seasons of job loss, financial unfairness, physical challenges, relational implosion, and family drama. We agreed early on that we wanted to travel the world together and had goals to visit Europe before we had kids. We could not make this a reality, no matter how much we trimmed our budget each month. However, this is where the journey gets really exciting. Instead of focusing on the unattainable, we focused our attention on the areas to which we could travel by car and subsequently had a blast, exploring from St. Petersburg, Florida, to the outskirts of Texas, and everything in between.

Are you building fun into your schedule? Are you making time for what's truly important in life? Time is precious, and we cannot control the amount that we'll be given. *Carpe diem* (seize the day) is my favorite catchphrase from the Robin Williams film *Dead Poets Society*. Seize every moment, and don't let a day go by without thoughtfully planning how to maximize the day to the fullest.

Grab the hand of the person you love most, and go off the grid— disappear for a while. Never stop dating her. Never stop the pursuit. I promise you'll never regret that decision.

Chapter Questions

- How do you think sitcoms, movies, magazines, and media showcase marriage?
- What are your personal hobbies? Where are you on the continuum—doing them too much or too little?
- What do you enjoy doing *together*? How often are you doing it?
- How can you energize your dating life and put more fun back into your schedule?

CHAPTER 2
The Value of Breaking Up

—Kate

Blessed is the home where each puts the other's happiness first.

—Unknown

The definition of *hard* is that it is solid and resistant. It is inflexible and requires a great deal of effort. It is exhausting, backbreaking, and laborious; it is uphill and even a Herculean effort. I don't know about you, but that word should not be anywhere near describing my marriage. I would like you to delete that word when it comes to your relationship. Just eliminate it. Just like you should remove the word *divorce*.

I was born with a "disadvantage" (at least most people in society would say so). I will never be in professional pictures or modeling. I will never be on Broadway in an important role. I could never cross the monkey bars on my own. And I had to learn how to button shirts, breastfeed my children, and open jars in a different way. My left hand has no bone or fingers past the first knuckles.

Despite this, most people I first meet never notice. My parents never treated it as a disadvantage or disability, and I learned to tie my shoes, and even play the piano at the age that everyone else did. I didn't know I had it "hard" at all. College papers were tedious work on a computer, and some people were outright cruel as I grew up. Those difficulties and experiences were opportunities for improvement.

So many people use their health, their pasts, and their disabilities to keep them from trying or doing things. I decided on a different tactic. I believe when we are faced with challenges and rise above them, we create a better version of ourselves—even better than if we had been "normal." Overcoming some simple tasks and some even harder ones has created who I am today. It has shaped me in incredible ways, and I am grateful. I hope that whatever you see as hard in your marriage, you will look at it as a launching place for exceptional growth in your relationship. You are capable of far more than you think.

God can and does use everyone who is willing. I pray that this is my story. And I pray even harder that this is your story in your marriage. What obstacle are you using as an excuse?

Let us take hold of courage and dive in, choosing greatness in everything that encompasses our romantic lives. Whatever your relationship handicap is, I know it possibly can be your greatest asset—if you let it!

I have many friends who have babies the same age as one of my own. At one point, in a desperate attempt to have some adult conversation one day, I scheduled a play date with the baby of one of these friends. It was rather silly because our children couldn't even crawl at the time, but we used it to create space for each other. I set out the coffee mugs, and she brought over gluten-free brownies. As the babies played on their little mats and chewed on their fingers and the dog's toys—complete accident on my part; why do baby toys and dog toys look so much alike?—we sipped our tea and talked.

She got into the muddled waters of her relationship, and at the time, it was very rough seas. She was tired, not getting enough sleep, and making some assumptions. She went on and on about everything that was wrong and got darker and gloomier the more she talked. I decided I had to act fast to salvage our play date. So I gave her my best advice.

"Girl, breaking up is key to the success of your marriage. You have to break up in order to thrive."

Her eyebrows raised into her hairline, and I think she may have choked on her brownie—I was dead serious. I tell the same thing to all my friends, especially women. Of course, they all stare at me like I have lost my mind and need serious help. I am fully aware this is a big thing, and from the world's perspective, it might be perceived as crazy, but it is relevant. This idea (and those that follow, below) may be the most important concepts our generation wrestles with.

You Must Break Up from Your Kids

Your kids more than likely came after your wedding ceremony, but even if they didn't, they must *always* be prioritized after your marriage relationship. I don't care if you have an eight-month-old miracle baby and you are still nursing him—get a babysitter! Break up with that child. One day, that kid will yell at you, go off to college, marry another, and create a new family. Where will you be with your marriage? The best advice we ever got on this subject was from a couple who didn't have children. We took their advice because they were on the outside and could see stuff that those of us with kids couldn't see. We were in it, we were blinded, we were tired, and we were busy. It was the best advice. *Make sure your marriage always stays in front of your kids.*

I am a mother to a miracle child, whom we call our bonus baby. I had high-risk pregnancies with both children, and we are lucky we have them at all. They are my pride and joy; my personal and very special bonuses in life. My dream in which I cried and deeply feared never was a reality. And I became a lioness when they were born—no one could care for them the way I could. If I had not taken this advice to heart, I know that Steve and I now would be in a challenging spot.

Men humbly take a back seat when babies come, and they do it ever so graciously. Nursing and healing our bodies take a drastic toll on us, and our men stand close by in great respect. However, our marriages must come first. I have heard of stories from women who say that sex is not a priority for extended months after giving birth. Ladies, that is manipulation. Your babies will be better off when you prioritize your husband and your sexual needs. Your marriage can be a thriving, dynamic, and energizing machine while raising children. When the kids eventually leave home, you won't be devastated and unaware of what to do with yourself. Trust me; you and your spouse will be much better parents for putting each other above all other relationships, including your children.

> Her children rise up and call her blessed; her
> husband also, and he praises her.

—Proverbs 31:28

You Must Break Up with Screen Time

Screen time is what we call anything from your phone to laptops, TV, movies, gaming systems, and social media platforms. You must break up with all of these. According to NewYorkPost.com, people spend more than two entire weeks of their lives on Instagram alone, and Netflix is actually a deterrent to sex.[1]

The average shut-off times for TV is now closer to 11:30 p.m., compared to 8:00 p.m. in the sixties. Children aged five to sixteen spend an average of six and a half hours a day in front of a screen, compared to three hours in 1995, according to market research firm Childwise. It is true that technology is not going anywhere, and there are more TVs than people in houses now. These statistics don't even touch the subjects of desensitization and pornographic issues (more on that later).

Screen time does not have to cause major issues in your marriage. You have to choose a board-game night, instead of a phone night. You have to

---

[1]

get the TV out of the bedroom. To this day, we are giddy when we stay at a hotel on vacation, where we can lie in bed and watch a show. We never do this at home! You also have to eat a meal without the phone in your hand or beside your plate. We're also training our kids in this, and they will call us out if we forget.

One day when our daughter was a toddler, she was on the floor, playing with some toys, when Steve came home from work. I quickly pulled out my phone to check on a phone conversation that my family had sent hours earlier. Steve had been offline for the past hour due to traffic, and he wanted to make sure there was nothing pressing with work that needed his attention. I glanced up and noticed both of us on our phones—and Amberly was looking at both of us with an inquisitive yet confused look on her face. My heart sank in that moment, as I realized this was not the message I wanted to send to my family. No piece of plastic and metal would come between or distract me from the ones I treasured most.

Every day, you have the choice to engage in the activities of your family. The value of your physical presence and focused attention is worth its weight in gold. In our digital world, it is easy to be physically present but mentally and emotionally detached. Don't deceive yourself into thinking you're involved when you are really on the sidelines. Your spouse and kids know full well when you are present.

Sally Clarkson says it perfectly:

> It's easier sometimes to tell myself, "We do our devotions, we go to church, they memorize scripture. That's all they need. I do enough." But it's not enough. What they really need is my life, my heart, my touch, my love, my patience, my correction, my gentleness, and my encouragement. They need me to be able to be there during the many teachable moments of each day, transforming them into discipline moments because of my spiritual intent for their lives.

It's simple. Be faithful and reliable to what God has entrusted to you. Find the balance, and don't cross the line. Ignore the distractions, and be engaged.

Steve and I pick multiple nights a week when we don't use any technology. We talk, play games, read together, or sit on the back deck. We know people who get in their hot tubs to change the routine to deter screen time. Other couples go out to restaurants that don't have TVs. We will often pick nontraditional date nights, like kayaking, indoor skydiving, or going for a run together. It's easy to revert to technology as the go-to for relaxation after a long, hard day. We all do it. Many of us don't have anything left in our tanks. Changing this one issue with technology, however, can change the trajectory of your entire marriage!

When we were first married, we had no money, and Netflix was still sending movies to us via snail mail—streaming was not yet available. We hijacked the internet from the clubhouse across the street from our apartment, but to do this, we had to be on the porch steps. If it was raining, we had to forget it, which was really a blessing in disguise. We didn't realize this until much later, when screen time started to creep into more everyday things.

Technology was a slow adaption process for us. Those of us from the 80's generation have gone from the first computers entering our homes all the way to speaking to our houses to close the garage or turn on music. Every single one of us should be evaluating and thinking of what we are going to allow in our life when it comes to technology. Devices in every room have become mainstream and social apps are replacing real social settings. Are you creating room for authentic conversations and deeper relationship?

I have a habit of forgetting my phone for hours, but then right before bed, I feel the need to check everything. It is crucial to carve out specific times to manage technology in a positive way and to enjoy it for what it offers. The point is, we still go back to the basics, and we do it often. We choose real "face time" over screens.

Choose the living, breathing soul waiting right in front of you. Push stop on the remote; put down your phone; come upstairs from your basement computer—it all can wait. Your spouse may not.

You Must Break Up with Your Extended Families

We love our families. I come from a big, loud, German-background group. We always had each other's backs, gave our opinions (whether wanted or not), and always wanted to know what was going on. We still have serious fun and are just plain crazy all the time.

I married into a family of people I would have been friends with, even if they weren't family. I know I am a lucky duck. I love them that much. Some of our biggest issues in marriage, however, have always involved the extended parts of our families. Tragically true and brutally honest, this is all too common when the topic of extended family is discussed with the numerous couples we sit down with. I like to believe that Jesus dealt with some of this as well. More than half of his family didn't believe in him or his ministry until after he had left this earth. There had to be some tension there.

Extended family relationships really surprised me. After all, our extended families were all Christians who wanted the best for each other. How could it hurt so much to leave and cleave correctly? I had to learn to step back from my family of origin and to create strong boundaries with Steve's extended family as well.

This boundary line is really hard for many of us to learn. We thrive on connections, and boundaries, at first glance, may seem to be severing those connections. Trust me; good boundaries help you build healthier relationships. If we are ineffective in setting limits with others, we are, in fact, choosing the opposite of loving well. We are creating unnecessary relationship stress and a lack of loving completely. Boundaries create healthy limits, so that we may stay connected correctly.

Each of us will be different in this. Some of us can talk to our mothers every day, and it is not an issue. Others of us talk to our mothers twice a month, and it's not a healthy thing. Find out where you need to draw the line.

The analogy of a plant is wonderful when looking at the topic of extended family. Let us say your marriage is the plant, and your extended family is the water. Water is life-giving. Not enough water and your plant withers and dies. However, if you overwater your plant, it will drown. Has the Christmas dinner tradition become too hard to maintain with a baby? Is the pressure to be somewhere or do something causing friction? Do you speak negatively about your spouse to your sister because you need an outlet? No more.

You Must Break Up with Your Work

I wanted Steve to write on this topic because he follows this advice very well. We discussed it multiple times, however, and he felt it would be more relevant coming from me. Why? Because I am the one who needs to be reminded of this.

My husband is amazing at prioritizing and wearing different hats in life. He knows when it's family time. He knows what career opportunities to take on and which ones to bypass. If he can't see a work/rest balance in his business, then it isn't for him. It's that simple.

It has been more difficult for me. For those of us in the bracket of Millennials and beyond, most women work outside the role of wife. We wear the hats of wife, mom, entrepreneur, teacher, blogger, and executive, sometimes making more than our husbands.

I love that women and men have a more side-by-side role now and that women have so many more opportunities than in years past. It truly makes my heart happy to know the road that is being paved for my son and daughter. In order to fully grasp this reality, we must all get over the mind-set that we can "copy and paste" the time of our parents' generation. It's incredible to take notice of, look at, and be mentored from the mind-set of the previous generations (what to do and what not to do), but we cannot look to those previous generations and expect to win in our *now*.

Long gone is the nine-to-five workday. It is more like 8:00 a.m. to 7:00 p.m. with travel times. Often we work from home, causing further blurring of the lines. We deal with ideas and concepts that the previous generations didn't deal with, and for us to expect to treat it the same way our parents did is just plain silly.

Bob Goff, author of the best-selling book *Love Does*, spoke at a conference, encouraging the men there to write their job-resignation letters and then give the letters to their wives. If, at any time, a wife felt that work and rest was out of balance, she had permission to send the resignation letter to her husband's boss—a very bold move. I would take it a step further. Both parties should write resignation letters. Even if the job is stay-at-home parent, if work is the first priority, then it is time to resign.

I heard about a hospice nurse who made notes about the last things people said in life and their number-one regrets. The most common regret was that they worked too much and didn't spend enough time with loved ones.

For me, as a lifestyle coach, blogger, and stay-at-home mom, I thought the topic of work was irrelevant for me and that I'd be speaking primarily to those individuals working outside the home. According to the Department of Labor, 70 percent of women work outside the home. This statistic does not include individuals (like me) who are self-employed or those who are stay-at-home parents. Basically, we all need to hear this. Whether or not we work out of the home, many of us have a very hard time putting our work down.

I am constantly on the go. If I'm not thinking about a work event, I'm thinking about our child's school assessment, or I'm folding laundry while listening to a podcast. I can't forget about the haircut appointment, that the car needs to be cleaned out, or that the dog needs grooming, and I have to text my sister about that recipe I need—you get the idea.

We all need to learn to shut off our work—mommy work,

corporate-ladder work, or home businesses. Women working is not the problem. Men working is not the problem. Work is important and key to the way our world functions and grows. If work has the majority of your focus, however, *you* are the problem in this equation. Make your significant other the priority of what you're willing to spend overtime on. According to that hospice nurse I mentioned above, nothing else is worthwhile.

We live in an era where it is hard to stop, hard to wait, and hard to just be. Between Instagram, Facebook, Snapchat, Marco Polo video messaging, fantasy football, and real-time trivia, it is the reality we live in. The list of schedules, extracurricular activities, friends' birthdays, and kids' sports are also added to this list, on top of longer working hours and duel working families. The generation before us had limited exposure to these circumstances.

Our generation is paving a new road, with trying to balance social media, sharing family roles, having home-based offices, and using global communications as the norm. We are called to share in the adventures of life with our spouses, and healthy, strong boundaries in these areas are key to making this happen. I won't tell you to cut all media and go back to a single family income, but we have to know where our boundaries are in our work lives. Do you know where that line is for you? Should you draw the line differently than you have?

I would love to say that my friend who came over for the play date decided to break up with all the issues that seemed to be staring right back at her. Unfortunately, it was a sad ending. Her kids still take center stage over her husband, and he knows it. She prioritizes progress in their financial status as more relevant than date night and intimacy. He believes football and late nights are more important than meaningful conversations and time with family. Not surprisingly, they like their friends more than they like each other, and they are sleeping in separate rooms.

Please hear our plea when we say these are important aspects to grasp and to implement. If you don't utilize the value of breaking up, these issues will break you.

If we are not careful, the adventurous pace we keep will prevent us from seeing the potential of our marriages and the amazing person right in front of us. When we are spinning out of control, we will never have the bandwidth for what God has laid out for us as the greatest gift. We were created to be a part of a team from the beginning of time, and you cannot be part of it if you are in another relationship, whether with your phone, your work, your kids, or even your extended families.

Chapter Questions

- What do you need to break up with?
- How are you going to break up with those things, and what are the strategies and systems you will put into place?
- Do you have boundaries in work? If so, where is your line?
- Is your spouse in agreement with these boundaries?
- Not having enough boundaries with your extended family can suffocate your marriage. What are the areas you need to release when it comes to extended family?
- If your spouse had access to your resignation letter, would he or she send it?
- What steps are you going to make to ensure that your marriage stays in front of the responsibilities of raising kids?
- How are you creating room for authentic conversations and deeper relationship?
- What are your boundaries when it comes to screen time?

CHAPTER 3

Easter Baskets

—Steve

Time is the currency of relationships. There's no way to
invest in a relationship without investing your time.

—Unknown

My family made several cross-country moves when I was growing
up. Everything changed several times for me—schools, sports teams,
neighbors, houses, friends, and proximity to extended family. I cycled
through eight schools in twelve years. My brothers were one of the rare
constants in life as we navigated the ups and downs of moving. As time
progressed, my older brother and I naturally gravitated toward each other;
it was rather easy. On the other hand, I viewed my younger brother as
a nagging little shadow, and we found ourselves more at odds with each
other than growing in friendship. It felt like mixing oil and water.

My parents strongly encouraged me to invest time in my little brother
and to find some common ground. We had to pick some things to do
together to reinforce that relationship—and we had to do that often. I had
to be very intentional at first, as it seemed forced—like I was just going

through the motions. But over time, it became natural and fruitful, and the friendship took on a whole new trajectory. The word *invest* literally means "to use, give, or devote one's time in order to achieve something."

Do you feel as if your romance is sometimes at a stalemate? Sure, you are married, but apart from the title, what are you achieving together? Over time, many couples find themselves standing figuratively with arms crossed, lines drawn in the sand, waiting for the other person to make a move in his or her direction. If we are not careful, we will become glorified roommates; pursuing separate careers; maybe raising a few kids; putting out occasional fires at work and home; dealing with chores, errands, and family demands; and pursuing individual hobbies. Life will become a blur. Yet over time, this becomes the all-too-familiar story of so many couples.

You want to know a little secret? Your spouse has the potential to be one of those rare constants throughout the course of your life. I say *potential* because it is not a guarantee. The choices you make from the moment you start dating until the day you say "I do"—and every day after that—will either strengthen or undermine that possibility. Hoping to grow in your relationship isn't enough. It takes action with purpose. It takes you constantly moving in each other's direction. One of my favorite sales managers always said, "Hope is not a strategy."

So what's the moral of the story? Stop keeping score, and move in your partner's direction. The scriptures tell us that love keeps no record of wrongs. If that's the case, then there is no reason for fuming, stewing, or quietly avoiding the issues because you've done your part—the longevity and fulfillment of your marriage could very well depend on it. Christ didn't love us because we first loved him. It was quite the opposite. He overextended himself and sought to bridge a connection that was broken. He infused love where there was estrangement, separation, and hostility. Christ demonstrated selfless love and calls us to do the same.

I encourage you to engage with your partner and develop skills that, over time, will become second nature. It doesn't happen overnight, but it will happen. A routine eventually becomes a habit, and a habit, over time, will define your character and you as a person.

Kate and I decided to push ourselves and run a half marathon a few years ago. We will never forget the feeling of crossing that finish line together. Due to that preparation, we can walk out the door and run a 5K without blinking an eye; no training is needed. We are conditioned now and our muscles respond accordingly. If you have developed unhealthy relational habits, then pressing the reset button initially will cause these activities to seem forced, just like it did with my brother and me.

Spring is a fun time of year, with so much growth and new life. Easter egg hunts are the best. I have fond childhood memories of egg hunts, as well as us kids wearing our white pants and plaid, pastel, button-down shirts. We would always do the hunt at our house before going to church. My brothers and I would scour the premises, finding every egg—or so we thought. Content with our prizes, we would sit down and begin opening the eggs. Our parents would calmly smile and give us that look that said there were more eggs to be found. What? More eggs? There was no way that we had overlooked anything. But we had. There were many that we had missed, even though we had been confident we had gathered all of them.

Most of us can be somewhat closed-minded and limit our imaginations in what our marriages could be. We simply do not know what we do not know. If you have not experienced a thriving marriage with your parents, extended family, or close friends, then it's hard to fully imagine what it could be and what *exceptional* could look like. False views of marriage are further fueled by culture, marketing, TV shows, cinema, and social media.

Are you possibly looking through a similar lens in your relationship? There is always more you can experience together, as a couple. Growth-minded individuals always seek more to put in their relational baskets.

People are not static creatures; they constantly change and develop. Kate isn't the same person I married over a decade ago. She came bundled with a unique set of interests and desires that have matured and shifted through the various seasons of our life together. So how do you protect yourselves from growing apart or waking up one morning feeling like the two of you are heading in separate directions?

The challenge today is that many couples are worn out by the end of the day, and energy and attention is waning due to careers, home necessities, bills, kids, family demands, media, and church activities. Some of us frequently catch up on the day's highlights but avoid the deeper conversations and interactions that lead to growth and greater romance.

As a salesman by trade, I tend to be the conversationalist between the two of us, and I can easily de-stress by talking. In our relationship, Kate adopts the "traditional" male role of not needing to talk in order to decompress. For her, less is more—not to mention that she has had two toddlers making constant chatter since early in the morning.

Some individuals love to talk and are never at a loss for something to say. Others may need a little more coaxing and encouragement to get the conversation flowing. I encourage both of you to find a middle ground and make it a priority.

Think back to when you were dating. Do you remember the sparks? I can play back these images like a movie. Do you remember how you feasted on every word the other said, knowing you were learning something knew about your newfound crush? Kate and I had a long-distance relationship for two years, which took a ton of invested time and effort to cultivate— we had to be more purposeful with the time we had. I remember staying up until all hours of the night, just talking and getting to know each other. We stayed up all night on a park bench at my college campus. I smile every time I see that bench. We thought we had only been talking for a few hours but then realized the light breaking over the clouds wasn't the city lights but was the signs of early dawn.

There was a constant adrenaline rush as we talked about virtually everything and hung on each other's every word, knowing we'd uncover new revelations about each other. From the very beginning, I desired to be a student of my wife, to learn and understand her, to observe and notice the subtleties that make her unique and special.

These are the cues that will help you connect with your spouse on a deeper level. Leave her an I-love-you note before work, bring her coffee in bed, text her during the day, bring home some flowers, or do the laundry when she's least expecting it. Maybe take the initiative on vacation planning this year, buy her a massage, take the kids for the day to give her a break, go shopping with her, try out a new restaurant, or light candles and turn on some soft music before she gets home.

This is your chance to tap into the core of your spouse and understand what is going on below the surface. You get the chance to express yourself in a judgment-free zone with your soul mate and the person you've chosen to do life with. These conversations might last five minutes or five hours. Regardless, you learn about each other and rediscover the art of vulnerability.

The greatest threat facing marriages today is routine. The busy patterns and schedules of your daily life will choke out and stymie any chance for growth. You may have to redesign, simplify, and shift some things around in order to move the needle from good to great. Deep down, you know this to be true. Don't let routine replace your romance.

What are you choosing to achieve in your marriage? We pray your invested time in one another creates greater growth, intimacy, impact, purpose, and passion. Go show the world something incredible and unique by how you invest the currency of your time.

I came across a powerful quote the other day: "Everyone has a friend during each stage of life. But only lucky ones have the same friend in all stages of life." Your spouse can be that friend. The one with whom you celebrate the peaks and valleys, the person with whom you sip hundred-dollar wine and boxed wine.

Reflecting back, I did not realize what was on the other side of my decision to invest in my younger brother. If I had done nothing, my relationship with him probably would have been average, at best. I learned a valuable lesson that has served me well in my relationship with Kate and has influenced the way I've chosen to invest time with her through the years. We are all holding Easter baskets in this grand egg hunt of life.

It's an exciting life, filled with endless potential and new discoveries. Will you consider that there is more out there for both of you?

Chapter Questions

- What do you want to achieve together?
- How do you protect yourself from growing apart or waking up one morning, feeling like the two of you are heading in separate directions?
- To what lengths would you go to ensure the stability of your marriage? What are three ways you can choose to invest in your romance?
- Growth-minded individuals always seek more to put in their relational baskets. What steps can you take to embrace this mindset?

CHAPTER 4

Build Your Tribe

—Kate and Steve

> The key to humanity's trouble ... has been to take and not
> give, to accept and not share, to grasp and not distribute.
>
> —Alice A. Bailey

We love talking with couples. We don't care if it's in a formal or informal setting. It is in and through these conversations that we have been sharpened and challenged and have had those "light bulb moments." We shared such a moment not long ago when the dialogue revolved around mentorship and the value of being mentored. Then the conversation shifted. It dawned on us that we were the next generation under this particular couple, and they made it abundantly clear that we had nothing to offer, that they couldn't learn from those "below" them, so they weren't going to focus on us unless we came to them for wisdom. Ouch.

We believe wholeheartedly in mentors. (In fact, we've devoted an entire chapter on this very thing.) Mentoring is foundational to the overall health of any relationship. It will truly make a good marriage great and a great marriage even greater! Let us be very clear, though—we disagree with the notion of disregarding the generation under you, simply because that younger generation is out of touch with your reality, and there are challenges with relatability.

We tend to take a stand on some key principles (or building blocks) that we firmly believe will lead to an incredibly life-giving relationship. One important and often overlooked idea is the mentee role.

The next generation coming behind you is truly amazing. They are doing and juggling more and arguably have more expectations on them to get it right than any other previous generation. They are incredible—think about all that they are managing and fighting against. Having the opportunity to see things from a younger generation's perspective has taught us as much as our mentors have.

We both have coached young pre-marriage couples through our church, and it possibly has been one of the biggest accelerators for our romance. Why? The topic of our marriage and how we daily engage is always in front of us. These young people constantly ask us about date nights, our communication and sex habits, and our growth as a team. Do not underestimate the power of the mentee role. We have to operate on a level of excellence when it comes to our romance because our mentees look up to us and ask about it.

In one aspect, mentoring has fostered accountability. In another, it is a constant reminder to dream together and talk about who we want to be and who we see ourselves becoming in the future. It's the journey of realizing our current and desired future state. Said another way, when you know people want to mimic your marriage and your ideas and want to be better at some aspect because of you, you will embrace personal responsibility in a beautiful and different way. You will hold yourself to a higher standard.

It doesn't mean we are perfect or have all the answers—far from that. In fact, we learn things all the time from the younger generations. (Hello, hashtags.) We are fortunate to witness the beginning of many marriages, due to our ministry. We are charged and ignited by the newness of love, passion, and commitment from the lenses of those beginning the journey. A fresh perspective from the starting gate of anticipation can be priceless.

> It became by mission to work with young people to help show them the way, not save them! But help them understand that there are choices that can be made today that will make the difference for their rest of their lives.

> —Jose A. Aviles, EdD

Contribution is key. Great things happen when you contribute to a cause or idea that is greater and beyond you. In essence, we extract more value from something or someone when we pour out into someone's cup, rather than being the cup-holder. In our opinion, building your legacy is not about buildings, money, empires, or even influence. It is about people. Period.

Many of us have incredible ideas, but it takes a multitude of people to make something magical happen. It takes a village to raise a child, reformers to create a movement, and an assembly to have a revival. The first step is in the mentor role. What good is it to have an exceptional romance, yet fail to share it with others so they too can benefit? We believe that by sharing that idea, we can change the shape of marriages and families all over the world for greatness and for God. Look at Jesus as an example. It only took one man who embraced God's plan, along with twelve imperfect mentees, to shape the entire future for the world. Become part of something bigger than yourself, and help and learn from those who are behind you.

We led our first small peer group a few years ago. We had settled into our community but really wanted to find other like-minded couples with kids in our same stage of life. We had no shortage of mentors and had a constant flow of younger couples in our life. If we had to pick the top five people with whom we were spending the most time, it would've been our kids, some family members, and work colleagues. But none of them was in the same stage of life as we were. We were on a quest to fill a void, knowing full well the importance of walking through life with peers.

We have seen this demonstrated in our own family due to our having several siblings who are in the military. We have watched this community of couples and families instantly connect around the military base. It seemed that overnight, they had support and friends who could relate to the here and now in their lives. These families were able to assist each other on the terrain of raising families, keeping the faith, maintaining marriages through long distance, and holding each other up in the most challenging situations. This doesn't just happen; it is cultivated. We encourage you to find those people who can create that safety net under you while you soar through life.

This has been a core value of ours since the beginning of our marriage. Our church often asks who will notice if your attendance becomes intermittent or if you decide to stop attending altogether. It's a great question. We like to press couples to analyze their own lives and determine if they are living connected or are insulated? Let's flip it now to your marriage. Aside from your spouse, who can hold you accountable, know when you're missing the mark, encourage and pray with you in the challenging times, celebrate the victories, and know the true and vulnerable you?

We believe most people see the fundamental value in friendship, but we see many people who are confused and wrestling with this notion of true friendship, with the current mirage of social media "friends." In today's culture, there is a lot of one- and two-dimensional communication. One-dimensional would be things like email or texts, where it is all words. Two-dimensional would be a phone call, where both words and tone can be expressed. So much of daily communication is done this way—it's the quickest and easiest way to stay connected with our hundreds (if not thousands) of contacts on Facebook, LinkedIn, Snapchat, Instagram, and others. Three-dimensional communication is by far the best and most impactful, albeit more time-consuming, and at times it's more difficult to maintain consistency. Being face-to-face allows you to express not only words and tone but also body language.

We now have analytics on our phones that show the amount of time we've spent on certain apps during any given week. We have done this sporadically to make sure we are walking the walk and not just talking the talk. Some folks have admitted to spending fifteen or more hours a week in social surfing on specific apps. Question: what if you traded in just half of that time for relevant, engaging, face-to-face connection with like-minded friends? It has made a huge difference for us. Make no mistake; social media will be the biggest competition for true friendship in our generation and those that follow. Striking the right balance is paramount.

To illustrate the point, we both have siblings who are currently serving in multiple branches of the armed forces. Maybe you have family or a close friend who has had to endure overseas deployments. If so, you might have heard comments from older generations that current military have it so much easier now due to the advancement in technology. We couldn't agree more. Skype, FaceTime, and other applications have literally revolutionized global communication. We have watched or attended countless sporting events that have showcased live feeds from remote parts of the Middle East and around the world, to pay tribute to and celebrate our military. This concept is simply incredible when you think about it.

While the modern soldier doesn't have to communicate only by snail mail, the additional technology has not solved all of the problems of physical separation. Our brothers have told us countless stories of deployments where their children would be more upset, sad, or irritable after a FaceTime call simply because they could not understand where Daddy was. They were frustrated. They would look behind the screen and struggle to rationalize how they could see and hear but not touch.

You cannot substitute physical presence. Relationships will hit a ceiling without it. Look no further than Tinder, Bumble, Badoo, Christian Mingle, or any other popular dating sites to drive the point home. Eventually, you must progress from messaging to an in-person meeting if you want the relationship to grow.

Most days, we are fortunate enough to walk our daughter and son to elementary school. A crosswalk helper stands there every morning and afternoon to greet all the kids, swapping high-fives and hugs. He takes a keen interest in their lives. Turns out he's run dozens of triathlons and marathons and several Iron Mans and has made a few appearances, representing Team USA across the globe for his age group. In a discussion one afternoon, he learned of Steve's swimming background and invited him to join his group twice a week to swim the lake.

Steve says,

I couldn't have said no if I'd tried. This group is composed of former Olympians and, in my book, athletic legends. I get the privilege of swimming with these men about once a week throughout the year. Almost a half century separates most of us in age, but we laugh, joke, and push each other every time we get together. They are all retired now and camp out at Subway after our workout, while I dive back into my busy workweek of emails, meetings, and forecast calls. Their kids are grown and gone, while mine are just entering kindergarten. They joke about their bodies tiring and fading, while I feel I'm just now hitting my stride. In one way, we're worlds apart. But I don't think about that when I'm with them early in the morning at the dock, as the sun is rising, and we're strapping on wet suits, caps, and goggles. We drift off from the dock and settle into our strokes and breathing rhythms. In these moments, I forget about the age divide and just think of them as friends. My life has been significantly enriched because of it.

So build out your tribe. Find someone a generation below you to encourage. Seek out peers to grow and share life together. Don't forget to build time into your schedule to have these meaningful relationships. And you never know—you might find those friends at a crosswalk.

Chapter Questions

- When was the last time you tried something new as a couple or took a calculated risk together?
- Who are two couples who could benefit from your story?
- We extract more value from something or someone when we pour into someone else's cup, rather than our being the cup-holder. With that in mind, how are you contributing to your marriage, or are you just consuming?
- Who comprises the peer group that truly knows you and your spouse? If one doesn't exist, what steps do you need to take?
- Social surfing has an impact on relational dynamics. Is this a problem for you? How can you grow the three-dimensional conversations in your life?

CHAPTER 5

Rubber Reaction

—Kate

Excellence is an act won by training and habituation … We are what we repeatedly do. Excellence, then, is not an act but a habit.

—Aristotle

We were married. The document was signed, the pastor paid, the garter tossed. Standing in the doorway of a pale-pink bathroom, in the basement of a red-carpet-covered church, the groom was asked to describe his thoughts on the day.

"Great, amazing, can't wait for the rest!"

I am turning fifty shades of red right now. I can't believe Steve decided that I was the one who should write on the topic of *sex*. Why me? Why not Steve? Especially with that answer on our wedding day.

The reason is that I have had the steepest learning curve in this department; I've had the most massive swings and growth in this area, so we felt I had more to share.

It makes me squirm that my three younger brothers will read this chapter—and my baby sister too. I am going to pretend she didn't get a copy of this part. Actually, scratch that. I wish I had gotten this advice much earlier than I did. I hope she does read it! I hope it changes her life!

I was raised with the idea that we just didn't *go there*—sex was shameful, and it was wrong to want and crave it. And I craved it. Physical touch is my number-one love language. (That I was not pregnant by fourteen was God's divine intervention and my grandmother's prayers!)

I was a Southern, homeschooled girl, raised in a medically correct and morally focused household. My mother was a registered nurse and Baptist girl who never drank. My father's mother was raised Catholic. Here is the thing: my mother and father did an amazing job of trying to overcome their awkwardness in talking to their thirteen-year-old homeschooled daughter about sex. Long gone are the days of relying on society and others to handle this correctly. You cannot push play on a tape recording or hand a book to your teen and expect the topic will be addressed for all of adulthood. There needs to be ongoing conversation and learning when it comes to this topic.

If you are turning five or twelve shades of red, or even if you think you have sex in the bag, keep reading. We have come a long way since the birds-and-bees conversations, but for many of us, it's still uncomfortable to talk about sex and especially in mixed company. I will try to make you laugh, give you fresh tips, and make this chapter exceptional.

> Let him kiss me with the kisses of his mouth!
> For your love is better than wine. (Song of Solomon 1:2)

My husband and I came to our marriage as technical virgins. We thought we were preserved the heartache of too many past relationships but we did have plenty of hurts and issues we had to work through. Wherever you are on the spectrum of what you bring to this topic, there is great hope. We want the topic of sex to be a place for every single relationship to come with great expectation and honesty, to dream of greater intimacy, and to have a bigger vision for what it can be.

Steve was once in a relationship where the other individual was not as decisive as I am. He actually trained himself to triple-check everything they did. When we first got married, I would get so mad about his doing that. He would ask me, question me, and then recheck if I was certain a dozen times, all before we followed through with anything. I had to continually encourage him that I said what I meant and I rarely changed my mind. On top of that, we had to learn about each other, learn about ourselves (we were only twenty-one), and learn about our bodies, all at the same time.

We have worked through a lot. On top of that, I was a late bloomer, who for the longest time was terrified of tampons. These were things I had to work through. As grown adults in married life, we should all be able to talk about sex. Do not let pride get in the way of being honest about a struggle you are having. Opening up could be the gateway for the most incredible intimacy you have yet to experience. Let's open up about what is comfortable, what is not, what we are dealing with, what we are okay with, and our expectations.

Men are told not to talk about these things because it is uncool to have any issues at all when it comes to sexual expectations, desires, or performance. They most especially shouldn't communicate any issues to the other person in the relationship; that would be considered emasculating. Whether it is pornographic images, not being able to perform, or hearing of their partners' struggles, they are told not to go there. In Christian circles, it's a step further, with the "How's your heart?" question versus just asking "Have you had sex with your wife recently?"

We make this so much harder than it needs to be. We silently suffer when everything could be cleared up very quickly with a few questions or explanations. Instead, we choose to stay silent around our significant other and our group of trusted peers, choosing to suffer, to stew, and to be secretive. Let's not complicate this. We need to ask the real questions on intimacy, even the hard ones. Working at understanding the deeper, more unique natures of each other will create the most incredible dynamic. It will give you freedom that you could only imagine in your wildest dreams.

When we first got married, I assumed I had to be everything for my husband, sexually. This is a major red flag. I ended up keeping ridiculous expectations for myself, fearing I would create the window of opportunity for him to stumble if I didn't keep him satisfied—and a lot. Because of that fear, I lied about my own enthusiasm with sex and made myself a sexual object.

This was not my husband's fault. He was very willing to talk about it, and he knew my heart wasn't in it. Obviously, I wasn't a very good actor, and my expectations were ruining all the fun. We had to rewrite this part of our romance just two years into our marriage. Because of that, I have some tips to share with you.

What I Would Tell My Young Married Self

• You are responsible for you.

Your body is his, and his is yours, but you are responsible for communicating about it correctly and telling him what you need from him. If he needs something from you, he is responsible for telling you. Trying to anticipate, guess, or be in front of it will only wear you both out and leave you unsatisfied.

• Make your bedroom a haven.

A woman told us before we got married to make sure we took time to make our bedroom nice. We just smiled and moved on. We wouldn't realize it till much later, but this was a golden key of advice. So often the bedroom is the last room we decorate, finish, and use. I know this to be a fact from personal observation. I was asked about bedroom drapes from a woman who finally was redoing their room, only after all of their children were grown, gone, and married themselves. It should be the opposite.

If you have to decide between buying a new coffee table or buying special sheets for the bed, buy the sheets! This is the haven for your marriage. It is the place to escape chores, work, electronic devices, and the outside world. For years—and I mean years—I would haul the laundry baskets into our bedroom. It was a constant reminder of what still needed to be done. My mistake was realized only after running ragged one day and coming upstairs to rest. There on the bed sat three loads of unfolded laundry. I could not even lie down.

I urge you to make this space work for you and your significant other. Let it speak to you and be soothing. There is nothing sexy about furniture that you both hate and piles of mail or clothes. Once I started seeing the potential this space had for us, I realized it could encourage connection. It could set the tone for our romantic life. I changed everything—no harsh colors, no clutter or distractions. Everything we had in the bedroom, we had to love. We upgraded the sheets, bought candles, and marked our visual space. No electronic devices became a mandatory rule. I still struggle with the habit of throwing all the clean laundry in the bedroom, but I am doing better, and that's done wonders for our marriage and romance.

- Ask about porn and image problems.

Every guy and girl has an image problem. If you live with any kind of technology, you know this is true. I am not saying every single guy acts out on seeing something sexual, or that every single woman watches *Magic Mike*, or that couples secretly use porn. We have images in front of us, however, every single day—most of the time, it's multiple times a day. Between explicit video gaming, soft-porn television shows, and social media platforms that show off body builders and bikini bodies, the issue is in our faces regularly. Image and visual stimulation is a part of our culture, and unless we live under a rock, we all come in contact with it. Sexual images that you don't talk about can create certain thoughts that can spiral into unhealthy habits, lack of personal confidence, distorted body expectations, sin, and pain for both parties, not to mention that it diminishes other people's true value.

The first time we ever talked about this, my husband started the conversation. He chose to tell me he had walked away from a strip club.

Every other man that he was working with had gone to the strip club. He talked about how the pressure had made him feel he was missing out.

I failed miserably at this conversation. I was embarrassed to talk about this issue. I was raised to believe that Christians are supposed to have self-control and not admit to even the thought of the thought.

"What do you mean you kind of *wanted* to go because everyone else went? Would you jump off a building if they all did that?" (Not my best moment.)

We are more saturated than ever before with what is deemed as acceptable now. This has to be discussed. Eventually, our being open about the struggle that is constantly in front of us was a very freeing conversation. It empowered us. Steve forever talks about it to others.

- Choose to have a no-shame/no-blame policy.

When someone opens up to you on a sexual topic, don't shame or blame him or her. The goal is open communication, not to create walls of isolation. However, we are called to hold each other accountable, and we achieve this by being accessible and vulnerable. The opposite of holding each other accountable is one of us shaming the other. It's possible he or she will never approach you again, if embarrassed, and he or she may silently struggle to a dangerous zone. We need to be *the* safe place for one another. This allows us to overcome challenges and insecurities as a team. This can be sexy, in and of itself.

So there Steve and I were, cruising along on the topic of sex, and we decided to try to have a baby. It sounds awesome in theory; the truth was a nightmare. That time in our sexual relationship was the absolute worst. (I haven't gone through menopause yet, but it was the worst yet.)

Planning intimacy around ovulation kits and every other night for optimization was not sexy. It didn't light my fire or his. To top it off, I took hormone pills to try to force cycles, so I could plan correctly and even lie on my back and stand on my head afterward. (Go ahead and laugh. It just wasn't fun.) I skipped two Mother's Days, and I cried every month. We did finally get pregnant and then learned I was considered high-risk.

Our little miracle baby came, and life was forever different. Life was better and harder all at the same time.

Sex Advice I Would Give My Married Self While Trying to Have a Baby

- Enjoy the process, no matter the outcome. Life throws curve balls, and this can be one of them. Whether there are babies, or adoptive babies, or no babies, or a combination of all, God has it. You do your part, and leave the rest alone.
- Talk to someone other than your spouse about the battle. I kept this painful journey close to my chest for a long time and didn't share much. My mother didn't know until years later. The few people who did know about my struggle had no understanding of where my head or heart was. Be open about this. I was shocked by how many other couples battle these same issues and feelings.
- Consider your spouse's feelings.
- Deal with the emotions of loss (counseling is advised).
- Go on vacation. This is, hands down, the best sex advice. You can relax, focus on each other, and rest. And a focus on playing and having fun always sets a different tone. You get out of your routines and ruts, and it's just plain awesome.

Our sweet children came back to back after this challenge, and we learned to tread water really well in the sex department. Here is what I would say to someone after the completion of the family unit. Whether you have none, two, or twelve by adoption, this sex advice still applies.

Advice for an Awesome Sex Life after Babies

- Have more sex! Super simple, but are you implementing this? The kids are sleeping through the night, and they love their babysitters. Your family is complete. Time to buckle down on some of the pleasure again. Spice it up. I heard once that every child added to the family unit creates three times the relationship strain on a marriage. You need to make sure you and your spouse aren't living in a roommate situation. Being partners in parenting isn't the only thing you should be partnering.

Children are a blessing, a true privilege—our story is testament to this—but I know when we are low in the area of sex. I can feel it. I don't keep charts or schedules or a count, but I am firmly aware when we are not in our normal rhythms. Chances are, you know where you are on this scale too. Are you low, doing okay, or knocking it out of the park?

- Date often. A healthy marriage creates joy, security, and confidence for all parties.
- Make a "sexy jar." We tell every couple that we can about this idea. People love it! It works, and it is such fun. (Sex should be a great time, by the way.) Grab a jar, some paper, and a pen. Tear the paper into thin strips, and divide them between your spouse and you. Write out fun things you want to do—like massages, kissing in the rain, or positions to try. Agree on all of them before you put them in the jar. When things get boring or ruts start happening, pull out a piece of paper, and do that by the end of week.
- Make sure you consider all contraceptive choices *before* romantic getaways! My husband and I planned a special getaway to the beach after our first child was born. She was still so little that we could cart her everywhere. We were so excited. We got a little condo within walking distance to the beach and our own private porch off the master suite. Have you ever packed for a trip with a two-month-old? How in the world can an infant have so much stuff?

We were so excited to be refreshed and to start our fall season with a new perspective—an after-baby honeymoon, so to speak. I even brought candles and massage oils. We failed epically. We failed to plan for proper protection. I have no words. Maybe we were still sleep-deprived or delirious from all the baby clothes, but in retrospect, we have laughed about this till we cried. It was not, however, a laughable matter at that time. Let's just say we both found out that we are highly sensitive to certain kinds of latex.

• Make self-care a priority for both of you. My husband is such a servant, and there was a season when he was working all day. Then he'd come home to help with our little ones. Weeks went by before he looked up. He was in need of some serious golf therapy and a few naps.

  I am passionate about optimal health for optimal living. I personally know the benefits of healthy living and body care. I also have experienced the opposite. I have eaten too much sugar, had too much weight on my hips, had too much to drink, pushed my body to stay up well past midnight to finish reading a book. I also have ignored my body too many times to count, pushing it to extremes.

  The wife does not have authority over her own body but yields it to her husband. In the same way, the husband does not have authority over his own body but yields it to his wife. (1 Corinthians 7:4–5)

This scripture was very freeing for me when I finally understood it. In all honesty, my husband appreciates my body in ways I never have. Steve sees me the way I want to be seen. He knows how much my body has gone through (as someone with a handicap, as an athlete with certain health issues, and with having had two high-risk pregnancies). He honors me when he acknowledges that and the beauty my figure holds for him. I am the same for him. We are mirrors for each other in the best way.

You are not your own. You were bought at a price and that price was God's Son. When you see that and know that in your bones, your desire to take care of yourself goes up. Your health impacts your relationship because when you make your health a priority, your energy, mood, sex drive, and patience are extremely high.

I tell Steve all the time, "You have to live to be one hundred. Make wise choices."

People laugh when they hear it, but it is an encouragement that I love him and I want him to thrive. I treasure our time, and I want to enjoy all of life (Lord willing) as a team. Being a good steward in this area is crucial to longevity in your marriage. Make it count.

Give each other this gift. Work out, eat right, and take the much-needed time away to refresh. Don't expect quid pro quo. Just give each other the gift of rest, recovery, and reciprocity.

- Schedule the number of times you want to have sex for the week. Some people schedule sex; others like to be spontaneous. We have found scheduling takes away the excitement and fun; it becomes routine and is not spicy in the least. Not scheduling sex, however, means busyness and exhaustion take over, and then it doesn't happen as often as we had thought it would. Our answer to this problem is simple. Schedule the number for the week. Do not set an exact day. If you have your number set, when the end of week comes, you will know if you hit your mark or if you need to get busy.

Family life can interrupt sex, or you can allow it to create a fire of intentionality for more sex and intimacy. Stephen and I have had the beautiful benefit of making sex a big priority in our life, and we have loved doing so. Tired, exhausted, or busy, it doesn't matter. Owning sex as a priority is mandatory to making an exceptional relationship. If you don't have any physical reasons that prevent you from sharing intimacy, it should be one of the top priorities and joys in your life.

The Best Advice to Reignite the Sexual Side of Your Relationship

It should always take two. I know that sounds lame, but many people we have talked to have said they handle this through masturbation and secrecy. It has become the norm for couples to privately use sex toys and to manage their satisfaction in the shower and alone. It has become normal, even in Christian circles, for women to talk about getting their satisfaction away from their husbands, and it is commonplace for "guys to be guys."

We decided early in our marriage that the sky was the limit and that being creative and open about what we wanted or needed was mandatory—and that we would always do everything together. Period. The end.

I know of a woman who said her husband had not completed the job for her the night before. She was tired, and it was late, and she liked it in the morning anyway, so they just went to sleep. But then she was talking about secretly handling things while he was at work the next day, all by herself.

My heart broke. I asked my husband how he would feel if he found out I'd talked about this to another girlfriend. He said it would crush him, not for what I'd done but because I hadn't included him. This woman was cutting her husband out of her sexual fulfillment, probably one of his greatest joys.

I have another friend who says her husband "handled" himself because she didn't have the energy for it. She also stated that it didn't bother her. Her reasoning was that she didn't have to mess with it, and he wasn't having an affair.

> You cry out, "Why doesn't the LORD accept my worship?" I'll tell you why! Because the LORD witnessed the vows you and your wife made when you were young. But you have been unfaithful to her, though she remained your faithful partner, the wife of your marriage vows. Didn't

the LORD make you one with your wife? In body and
spirit you are his. (Malachi 2:14–15)

What does this really mean? To be blunt, if you hop in the shower for
a little happy ending, your significant other should go with you. It might
sound really old-school, but this choice is the very best choice. It creates
intimacy with and fulfillment for each other. When sexual acts are done
in secret and alone, we are not letting the other person fulfill this need for
us in the way God intended. We fail to connect in our sex lives because
we are not being honest. Let me be very clear again: everything we do,
we do together. If we can't do it together, we don't do it.

Are you choosing TV over your marriage? Are you secretly handling
your sexual needs? Where are you investing in this? Where are you having
fun, prioritizing, and dreaming? If it is not your marriage, it is something
else. Personally, we have found nothing else is worth it.

> Drink water from your own cistern,
> running water from your own well.
> Should your springs overflow in the streets,
> your streams of water in the public squares?
> Let them be yours alone,
> never to be shared with strangers.
> May your fountain be blessed,
> and may you rejoice in the wife of your youth.
> A loving doe, a graceful deer—
> may her breasts satisfy you always,
> may you ever be intoxicated with her love. (Proverbs
> 5:15–19)

Chapter Questions

- Are you choosing TV, work, hobbies, or kids over your sex life in any way?
- Are you low, doing OK, or knocking it out of the park with your sex life?
- Are you initiating sex in the bedroom? How can you do better?
- What is your weekly number, and does your spouse know it?
- What is one sexual desire or need you want to meet for your partner by the end of the week?
- Where would you like your next "sexy-moon vacation" to be?
- Where are you really having fun, prioritizing, and dreaming?

CHAPTER 6

Keeping Boredom at Bay

—Kate and Steve

Make the most of yourself by fanning the tiny, inner
sparks of possibility into flames of achievement.

—Golda Meir

Kate is a lifestyle coach and former athlete. Steve has had a career in sales
and is a former athlete as well. We are all about efficiency and schedules,
but that can get boring really fast.

The discomfort of your routine can become a potentially painful
regret. It can become so monotonous that one day you will wake up and
cry out from the dullness that has become your life. Most of us accept
this as the new norm and status quo, while we're unaware of how we got
from burning passion to this. We crawl into the humdrum of routine and
settle in for consistency and average mediocrity.

This does not have to be you. This is not what you were made for. This
is not the standard to which you should hold yourself. We don't think God
would consider this as acceptable, and neither should you. We believe he

had something completely different in mind when he made man's partner in the garden of Eden.

We were made to be in God's bigger picture, and our marriages are the foundation of that. Making sure we are focused on developing our romantic dreams can keep us excited for creating something extraordinary. Stepping up and raising our standards to live boldly and fearlessly can create immense drive. How? You're either living life too fast or too slow. The pace of your marriage is crucial to creating excellence.

Are you so busy that you've lost your wonder and curiosity for what could be? When was the last time you paused just to give a soft kiss? How many times have you promised you would be somewhere or do something for your spouse or kids, only to allow situations to derail that commitment? Sure, there are always exceptions that cannot be avoided (like a flat tire, emergency, or sickness), but we're not talking about those. We're talking about the times you failed to prioritize, to watch the clock properly, to account for traffic, to close the laptop on time, or failed to tell someone else the word *no* instead of your spouse.

When you're exhausted from the normal speed of your existence, you may squash any potential for romantic fire. If you are so busy and overwhelmed in your day-to-day life that there is no margin for dreaming or engaging, then you likely will lose your zeal. If this depicts your current state, then you might have time only for flipping the television on—and maybe not even that. You may find yourself out of energy, unable to engage in anything. Game night, laughter, special plans for date nights, gifts, and deeper conversations have no place because you physically have no bandwidth.

On the flip side, perhaps your dreams are so slow in coming to fruition that you have lost hope of reaching it entirely. Some dreams are literally life dreams, and it takes a long time to make them happen. To wait it out is hard and sometimes daunting. Also, it is much harder if you are not focused on smaller dreams during the wait. For example, waiting for the dream of motherhood was a real challenge for Kate. She allowed it to be all-encompassing. It took over her everyday life, and with that, Steve got bored—bored of waiting for her to focus on anything else. Every other dream got shelved. The struggle in her heart was something indescribable. The ache of infertility was unbearable, confining, and rattling.

Women who go through this struggle never forget that feeling in the pit of their stomachs, the emptiness that invades every emotion. They focus entirely on getting pregnant, without thought of anything else. That's not healthy for any dream. There are seasons of focused time on certain goals, but it's a mistake to focus so much energy on a goal that you miss the people and blessings right in front of you.

Resentment has a way of weaving its way into your life in seasons like this. It may seem to you that others get to do something or have certain experiences, but you don't. Maybe you secretly blame your spouse for the situations you find yourselves in. You might think, *If _____ had simply done _____, then we wouldn't be in this situation,* or *If _____ had only listened to my opinion or had gone along with my recommendations, this situation wouldn't have happened.* This gets dangerous very quickly. A relationship that centers on keeping an even score is damaging as well.

We have a friend whose husband went on an international golf trip just weeks after she delivered their second child. Friends and strangers alike were shocked at their decision. She was heartbroken that so many people thought she should hold her husband back from a once-in-a-lifetime opportunity, just because it was not "fair." She also laughed that people said she *let* him go; it was more like she urged him to go. This is the type of chemistry that underscores a strong marriage. What do you do when the score is not even? Do you choose joy and encouragement or resentment and bitterness?

Things like joy, risk, euphoria, and emotional attachment fuel love. These things create a fertile environment for romance to blossom. The opposite is true as well. Routine, a sense of duty, resentment, and uneventful behaviors always lead to boredom.

Paying attention to the speed of life is also key when it comes to your dreams. What is your relationship speed? How do you operate the best? If you go at too fast a pace, you will replace energy with exhaustion and run out of steam. The ability to improve will be lost. You'll end up just running and have no idea where your course is headed. If the pace is too slow, you might lose hope completely and become bored.

We believe many couples become bored because they are on the wrong boat headed the wrong way. Many choose selfishness and other people's ideas over unity and God's plan. Our advice is to get out of that boat. It is not headed where you should be going anyway.

The Bible tells us that Jonah had this problem. He got in a boat toward a destination where he wasn't supposed to go. He was ill equipped for the journey and the storm. It took him down and everybody else with him. Before you lose everything, before you arrive somewhere you shouldn't be, throw yourself over and change course! Only then can you pause long enough to dream really big and fulfill your purpose.

Will a whale swallow you up? Maybe. You might need to be in a quiet place where you can disconnect from others for a bit. Take a few days and reevaluate, like Jonah did. Chart a different direction. Make it something incredible and worth living for. By doing this you could save yourself, your marriage, and everyone else in your boat.

We had a dream to go to Europe before we had kids, but financially, we just could not make it happen. We were frustrated. We knew this dream would have to die. Europe would still come but not before kids. To make matters worse, we were in the middle of a very trying process to start our family. We were low on rest and in desperate need of a vacation. Steve was also in a massive transition with work, and we lived far away from our siblings.

What do you do during transitions, when you're overwhelmed with needs, hurting financially, and waiting? We decided to take a road trip. The number-one tip we give couples who are struggling and going through hardship is to go on a vacation. When the pain of unmet dreams and hopes comes crashing in, planning time to deal with them in a different setting is always a great idea.

We changed course for our weekend and jumped out of the boat. With less than a week's notice, we scheduled a trip to visit Steve's brother and family in Clovis, New Mexico, where they were stationed with the United States Air Force. His brother was in between deployments, and it had been a long time since all of us had been together.

We drove well into the night and stopped at a rest stop at almost three o'clock in the morning. With a sleeping bag and a shared pillow, a Honda Civic, and little else, we made it all the way from Atlanta, Georgia, to Clovis, New Mexico, seventeen hours later. Sleep-deprived and hungry, we were ecstatic to see Steve's brother and wife, to sip wine, and to laugh. We were encouraged to be patient, despite our feeling of loss. We held their newest son in our arms, wrapped in blue blankets, and just cried. We were dealing with a setback in our dreams.

Our timeline wasn't God's, and the unfulfilled desires were painful. We were still in a one-bedroom apartment and paying off the last of our student debts. We had two car payments and very little in savings to do anything extravagant. Kate was working on Saturdays to keep us afloat. We just wanted to feel like we could breathe. That first night, we crawled into the extra bed in our nephew's room and prayed for different outcomes.

That trip remains one of the most refreshing trips we ever took. It was healing, and we realized it was time, like Jonah, to get our heads back in the game. For three days, we redirected ourselves back to what our life was supposed to be. We reminded ourselves that no matter what we thought it should be, we would be obedient and faithful in our now. We would trust God's goodness.

If you are hurting or going through a storm, we encourage you to get away. Don't brush it under the rug. Don't run from it. Go gain some perspective so that you can tackle life as a strong unit and maintain passion, despite it all.

During this season, we studied the apostle Paul, who spent the better part of his last days in prison. He managed to stay steadfast, despite beatings and other persecution. How could he write such passionate and inspirational letters while enduring so much pain? We believe it was because he knew the bigger picture—his purpose and the part he played.

Do you know the part you play in your marriage? Do you know the bigger picture? God said it was not good for man to be alone in the garden. It was the only thing "not good" before the fall of man. We were created for a connection with God and our spouses from the very beginning of time.

We decided to create a vision statement that we both could stand on for our relationship, so that no matter what—the ups, the downs, the storms, and the calm—we would hold fast. We didn't want excess. We wanted excellence. We wanted to continually create something exceptional in our life. We wanted to guard the good deposit that we had been given (2 Timothy 1:14).

Do you have a vision for your marriage? Is it written down? Do you both take ownership of it? Your marriage is a mighty privilege. You get to be a part of a great story. Knowing God's vision for your relationship is a cornerstone for thriving romantically. It is very hard to get bored when you have this vision in front of you.

For as he thinks in his heart, so is he. (Psalms 23:7)

After we created our vision statement, we created one-year goals. Then a mentor challenged us to make five-year goals. Creating visions and goals is one of the greatest habits for keeping routine from sabotaging your romance. Additionally, we made ten-year goals and a life-goals list (sometimes known as a bucket list). We also have a date-night list and a places-to-visit list. We regularly talk about how we can spice things up, and add, change, or even eliminate things if they no longer serve us.

Make sure you are always reaching and not settling. We bought our first house six years into our marriage and had our two children, back-to-back. We were happy and content, settled and comfortable. Suddenly, we were in a place where our dreams were exceeded. When you feel you have arrived, however, you may end up with vanity. This can be dangerous. You sell yourself short by being comfortable, which often leads to not reaching for a higher purpose or focus. You become grateful and then settled. More often than not, this eventually leads to boredom.

Many couples reach this in the middle of marriage - you are no longer a newlywed and not yet empty nesters. They might be doing better than their parents did, their kids are good kids, they have a good marriage, and they have decent jobs. While we were living this reality, someone challenged Kate by asking a very important question:

"Are you holding your family and your marriage back by choosing security over being stretched?"

Kate was floored and had no answer for this. There is a big difference between contentment and complacency. She had chosen the latter. She wasn't being stretched or pushing herself in any way, and she realized her mistake with sudden and sharp clarity.

When your dreams exceed the ideas you hoped for, how do you keep reaching and not settle? The answer is simple: raise your standards. So often there is an idea in our heads, and we emotionally and mentally can't move forward from the original vision. It's why many people are limited. It is called a closed mind-set. In careers, spirituality, and relationships, we stand behind the limiting beliefs that we have made for ourselves and conform to average. It is like the story of the circus elephant that never breaks the tiny rope holding it in place. It was trained as a baby that it was not strong enough to break it. It was true at the time, but now, as a grown elephant, it is no longer the truth. Yet the elephant stands there, still tied to that belief.

May you be empowered to step up and to identify where you can dream bigger and go further. Identify those areas where you can break ropes and where you can create energy, commitment, and joy for everything you walk through as a team. That, dear friends, will keep boredom at bay.

A Million Dreams

A million dreams are keeping me awake
I think of what the world could be
A vision of the one I see
A million dreams is all it's gonna take
A million dreams for the world we're gonna make
However big, however small
Let me be part of it all
Share your dreams with me

—Benj Pasek and Justin Paul

Chapter Questions

- How is busyness affecting your wonder and curiosity for what your romance could be?
- What is your relationship speed? How do you operate the best?
- What is your vision for your marriage?
  - Five-year goals?
  - Ten-year goals?
- How are you being stretched right now?
- What is an area in which you want to improve in your relationship?
- Do you know the part you play in your marriage by God's standards? Do you know the bigger picture?

CHAPTER 7

From Common to Sacred

—*Steve*

Your life is always moving in the direction of your strongest thoughts.

—Craig Groeshel

I had the opportunity to travel to Rome, Italy, with my music group to minister to some local churches during my sophomore year at Lee University. During our day off, the group took a tour of the Vatican, and it was spectacular. We maneuvered our way through the various hallways with tapestries, sculptures, and priceless pieces of art as we drew closer to St. Peter's Basilica. After passing *The Pieta* by Michelangelo, my eyes were drawn to the enormity of the church. I was overwhelmed with wonder at the sheer size, lavish beauty, and immaculate detail surrounding me.

In our wandering, my friends and I accidentally walked through a side door that was not intended for public use and entered a small chamber of sorts, filled with lit candles and gorgeous chandeliers. We noticed a parish priest, performing his duties. The silence and tranquility of the room stood in sharp contrast to the noise of the hundreds of tourist groups on the other side of the wall. We quickly tried to apologize in broken Italian and were about to turn and leave.

The priest, however, beckoned us into the chamber. He then sprinkled us with holy water and began to pray over us, first in Italian and then in broken English. Tears filled my eyes as his words sank into my soul, and I felt God's presence. I knew in an instant that it was a holy place. God's Spirit was there, and it demanded a certain respect, awe, and reverence. After blessing us, he sent us on our way. I will never forget this experience as long as I live. A valuable awareness about holiness and sacredness was impressed upon me that day.

One of my favorite Old Testament heroes is Daniel. Daniel was a prominent prophet from the Old Testament who emerged about six centuries before Christ. He was an accomplished politician. However, the Babylonian culture was contradictory to his own, and at times it was hostile to the devotion and customs of his Jewish faith. He was constantly persecuted, yet through it all, God was with Daniel and continued to prosper and promote him, despite his facing an array of challenges.

He was carried away to Babylon as a teenager during the exile in 605 BC, along with all the treasures from Solomon's palace and temple; he would end up living there for over sixty years. His Jewish homeland, culture, traditions, and way of life were desecrated and the Jews were scattered throughout the Middle East. The Babylonians had an immense empire to manage, so they chose promising young Hebrew men to groom into leadership positions. Daniel was one of these men. He initially served as a trainee for Nebuchadnezzar's court and then eventually as an adviser to foreign kings, as he was highly regarded for his wisdom.

During this time, the Babylonian throne was in a bit of flux due to several successions and some assassinations. We are introduced to a man named Belshazzar, who ruled for about ten years, during his father's absence from the throne. Belshazzar's life account is summed up in only one brief chapter.

It was not uncommon for kings to throw massive feasts and parties. It was a way to showcase their wealth, power, and prestige in a time where the divide in social classes could not have been any greater. Ironically, the punctuation point for Belshazzar's life and the way he will be remembered for eternity centers on a single night that was shared with over a thousand of his friends.

Who's your favorite Hollywood celebrity? Imagine that this individual was throwing a huge party after the Academy Awards for the Who's Who of Hollywood. Valet services would escort VIP guests from their expensive cars into the foyer of a sprawling Malibu mansion with views of the ocean. Friends, business associates, politicians, and other famous people would be walking the grounds. The place would be immaculately decorated with crystal, gold, diamonds, and high fashion. Manicured gardens, imported flowers, and exotic animals would be on display. Entertainers and famous musicians would take the stage throughout the evening. Tables would be filled with the choicest hors d'oeuvres, food, and wine for guests to enjoy. The grandeur and luxury would be beyond anything you'd ever seen.

A similar scene took place in Belshazzar's castle.

As the revelry continued into the night, Belshazzar had an idea. Why not showcase his dominance, supremacy, and power by taking something that was designated for sacrificial worship and using it for himself?

> So they brought in the gold goblets that had been taken from the temple of God in Jerusalem, and the king and his nobles, his wives and his concubines drank from them. (Daniel 5:3)

This was no accident, and Belshazzar was not ignorant. He had heard the stories of his grandfather Nebuchadnezzar and the humiliation he had experienced due to his lack of reverence for God (Daniel 4:33–37). Nebuchadnezzar had seen the power of God through visions and the miraculous saving of Shadrach, Meshach, and Abed-Nego from the fiery furnace. But Belshazzar disregarded all of this. His pride got in the way, and he made a choice to make sacred things commonplace.

God miraculously interrupted the party by sending a solemn

message to Belshazzar, and Daniel was called upon to interpret. Daniel communicated that Belshazzar's kingdom was finished; he had been weighed in the balances and found wanting, and his kingdom would be given to the Medes and Persians. That very night, Belshazzar was overthrown and slain, and Darius the Mede assumed leadership of the entire kingdom.

> But you, Belshazzar, have not humbled yourself, though you knew all this. Instead, you have set yourself up against the Lord of heaven … you did not honor the God who holds in his hand your life and all your ways. (Daniel 5:23)

These weren't just any goblets. These were created, crafted, and designed for the temple to worship and glorify God. They were purposely set apart from the world to be instruments for holiness. They had a specific purpose in the priestly routine for purification, sacrifice, and forgiveness.

We too, in the same way, were created in the image of God to be vessels through which he can pour his love, especially to our spouses. Each of our bodies is the temple of the Holy Spirit, and we've been instructed to honor God with our bodies. We have been crafted for a particular purpose as well.

> Do you not know that your bodies are temples of the Holy Spirit, who is in you, whom you have received from God? You are not your own; you were bought at a price. Therefore honor God with your bodies. (1 Corinthians 6:19–20)

Marriage is sacred, but culture has slowly eroded that foundation over the years. Given this phenomenon, Millennials and Generation Z are more wary of the trending divorce rate, and that has translated into their delaying marriage—or not getting married at all—due to fear, uncertainty, and doubt.

How you view and think about your marriage is crucial. Your perceptions mature into perspectives, which ultimately determine and define your frame of mind. Perceptions can be right or wrong, but if those perceptions are reinforced over time, they will eventually become what you believe. You are defined and shaped by your thoughts, and you ultimately act on what you believe. If inaccurate and misguided, these thoughts could formulate opinions that could be limiting, damaging, and potentially very hard to reverse.

Our society has not been ashamed or remorseful in making a public mockery of marriage. Many sitcoms and trending TV shows make it the subject of coarse jesting. They garner popularity by surprising and shocking viewers and pushing the boundaries of what is socially acceptable. Marriage has been a target. Popular songs glorify unabashed fooling around, sensuality, and the degradation of women. The media seems to showcase never-ending stories about infidelity and marriage scandals from our social elite, politicians, sports stars, and celebrities. How did we get here, and is there any hope of restoring God's original plan for marriage?

Recommit to viewing this amazing relational creation as a rare gift, a treasure from God, and something that can never be replaced. It's something sacred, set apart, and designed by the Creator of life to allow you to experience God's absolute best for you on this earth. Maybe if we get this right, we will be able to get a taste of heaven here on earth. Isn't that what you want for your marriage? God labeled the marriage relationship as sacred and gave it to us to unwrap and enjoy. We make marriage common when we don't view and use it for the purpose for which it was called.

But your perception of marriage doesn't just come from culture. It is shaped by your upbringing, family of origin, friends, and demographics. These are powerful influences that ultimately shape your frame of mind on marriage. You will have the tendency to look at marriage as common, disposable, and secular if you are intoxicated and under the influence of modern culture. Today's culture says to take marriage for a test drive, and if you like it, buy it. But if you begin to get tired of it or it starts to have problems, just trade it in for something else. Are you viewing your marriage with a lease mind-set, or are you all in, with a commitment to loyalty, longevity, and love?

We can draw another principle from this Bible story. Ironically enough, the Medes and Persians were sneaking their way through the city's underground tunnels while Belshazzar's party was going on. Where is the weakness within the walls of your marriage, and where are your senses deadened or numbed? We all need to be vigilant to protect our own relational fortresses. My hope is that you shift the way you look at your own marriage from something that is common to something that is sacred.

Your actions will speak louder than words. The way you respond to your spouse is out of reverence to God because that person sitting across from you is made in God's image. The King crafted your spouse. That is a big responsibility to get this right!

I'll close with a quote from A. W. Tozer's *The Pursuit of God*:

> It is not what a man does that determines whether his work is sacred or secular; it is why he does it. The motive is everything. Let a man sanctify the Lord God in his heart and he can thereafter do no common act.

The Vow

Today, I, _____, renew my marriage vows in the presence of God, in the name of Jesus Christ, our Lord, and in the standing power of the Holy Spirit.

_____, you and I have a treasured relationship that I view as a gift from God. I will accept you in your uniqueness; respect you in your differences from me; allow you room for individual expression; seek to understand and meet your needs; refrain from being overbearing and demanding; grant you the freedom to fail; forgive you for your errors; restore you when you stumble; bear your burdens when you cannot carry them alone; give thanks daily for you and pray for you; provide for your needs within my means; encourage the realization of your full potential; and remind you often, through word and deed, that you are the most important person in the world to me.

I renew my vow of commitment to you, to have and to hold, from this day forward, for better or worse, for richer or poorer, in sickness and in health, to love and to cherish, till we do part, according to God's holy sacrament; and thereto, I pledge you my faith.

Chapter Questions

• Perceptions can define your frame of mind. What was your perception of marriage growing up? What or who has been the biggest influence on that perception? Why has it been positive or negative?
• Where are the perceived weaknesses within the walls of your marriage?
• In what areas have your senses been deadened or numbed due to the intoxication of our current culture?
• How does believing in God's plan for marriage change your daily choices?

CHAPTER 8

Killing the Love Fern

—Kate and Steve

"It's our love fern! Oh, Bennie boo-boo boo-boo."

—Andie, in How to Lose a Guy in 10 Days

Kate says,

I don't remember why we were fighting. It was probably something about the trash or extended family expectations. It was obviously something silly and insignificant, something twenty-one-year-olds feel are really key—like how to fold towels the right way or not leave their boxers hanging on the back or the doorknob. Something of that nature was the reason.

I don't think Steve ever saw his mother raise her voice like I raise mine. I was raised in a big, loud, and vocal family. Opinions are not appreciated, but that doesn't stop any of us because we love each other furiously and are going to tell you.

With that in mind, just months into our marriage, we had an epic escalation. When I matched Steve's vocal capacity, I saw his eyes widen in shocked terror and utter bewilderment. He thought he could dominate by getting bolder and stronger. Ha! I knew I had him, and so I kept going. I ranted on and on. I said mean, horrid things, and I boxed him in good with my words. After all, I was a pro at this. I almost smirked in triumph that I was right, and he was going to get it. But of course, young, just married, and newly with each other, I was not in full knowledge. I was unaware of all that Steve had in store for me. I did not anticipate the sharp turn that this particular conversation would take for both of us, and I was at a complete loss when it did.

For the first time (and the last), my husband grabbed his keys off the chunky plastic wall hook and walked out of the house. It wasn't a calm exit, and it wasn't a silent one. I felt sick. This was not how it was supposed to go. I had not won the argument. In fact, I had lost ground in my own integrity, in our connection, and—worst of all—respect. I registered, after the fact, that I had never allowed myself to speak to another human being that way, so why would I talk to the earthly lover of my soul like that? I vowed that very week that my husband would get greater respect in my communication than anyone else. Because of who he is in my life, he deserved better, not worse.

I have heard of others say the reason your family gets to see the worst side of you is because they are closest to you, and you can drop your guard. I believe in authenticity, but I also believe in treating people like Jesus treated people. There was nothing of Jesus in the way I had communicated at that moment.

After that, we would both demand better in the way we talked to each other. We would communicate about everything and never stuff or hide it. There would be a gut-level honesty that no one else gets in our lives, but we would always try to speak to each other as if we were desperately, madly, over the moon about one another—because we are.

We don't do this perfectly. We are still more on the vocal spectrum than the avoider spectrum, but that day shifted us. No matter how heated we are or what is going on externally, I always want to be life-giving to Steve—like pouring water on a wilted fern.

In that silly, ridiculous fight, he had not gotten his point across either.

For me, when he stormed out, saying all manner of things, he was saying my anger and hurt were too big for him. I couldn't be handled because I couldn't be controlled. He wasn't going to stand by me, work it out with me, or even fight for me. It was crushing to a very deep level. My bones felt it that day. Do you know what I am talking about? Only a few things have happened to me that have impacted me in this way. Some of these things are incredible and amazing. Some of them are more devastating. There are certain moments that mark you. That particular fight was one of those moments for both of us.

In all of this, there is great hope. Realizing so early on in our relationship that we didn't want it characterized by this toxic way of communicating was a giant victory for our romance. We both had to change. We have made our home a place for respect for each other, and we even demand others do the same (or they can leave). It is that serious for us. I would not allow strangers to speak to Steve in a negative way without my defending him. Why, then, would I allow myself or those closest to him talk in such a way? For us, if we hadn't shifted very quickly, our fighting tactics would have smothered the very passion we love in each other.

There's a scene in the movie *How to Lose a Guy in 10 Days*, where the girl goes ballistic about a dead fern. The guy forgot to water it. It dies, and she completely loses her mind about it. She asks the guy, dramatically, while holding the dead plant, if he is also going to let their love die. The scene is hilarious. She goes nuts over the smallest things and uses them as grounds to head to a third-party mediator and counselor. It is funny because we all know the image is slightly true. It's all the little things that we put on a shelf, forget, tiptoe around, and don't "water" that can kill our relationships.

We know of some divorce lawyers who tell stories of the break-up point for relationships. Shockingly, many of them say the point of ending things is often over small stuff. Many of these things are so insignificant that it is hard not to laugh at the hilarity of the issues that come out.

It is amazing how many people will say that minor things are the dividing factor for the relationship. And that, my dear friends, is no laughing matter. It is true in our personal lives as well. Much of what tears us apart is related to the little things. It's the comment that a great-uncle said to you when you were eight, or the person at work who didn't think you could cut it, or that your spouse rolled his or her eyes when you described your dream.

For this chapter, we want to focus on the one thing that kills your romance the fastest and the four things that can help cultivate more passion and excellence.

The Number-One Killer

Focusing On What You Don't Like
Steve says,

My first major job struggles happened just a few short years into our marriage. We were married in 2007, and the financial crash was in '08. Business units were cutting teams constantly. I had no control over this, and, of course, being young and new, I was usually one of the first to go. They just assumed I'd bounce back faster because I was young. People don't want to take on a fresh-out-of-college new guy when times are hard. The risk is too deep. They need numbers, and they need them now. They can't wait on the young kid's learning curve. I lost and held over five jobs in six years. It was big, heavy stuff for an ambitious twenty-two-year-old with a wife.

Evenings were filled with complaining and verbalizing all of my frustrations to Kate. I would bring the drama from work into the front door of our apartment and it choked out the vibrancy of our life. She was so gracious but it wore on her a lot. It wasn't until years later that I fully understood the impact of my decisions to vent to this degree.

After this season, I thought I knew where work stood, and began learning how to trust God more fully. However, that was not the last of my job struggles. It would take me many more years before I learned to not allow the pressures and challenges to negatively infiltrate my every moment.

Kate says,

Years later, I watched him not even flinch when major shifting was going on in his company. My husband's faith in who he was and who God is was an image of tranquility. I saw how much strength he had because of those earlier years. We've been there. We know that no matter what, we could do it again. Worrying about it doesn't help anyone, and so he didn't.

Work was work—until it wasn't. It became his prison, and there was nowhere to get another job at the time. He was boxed in and being used. When I say it was bad, that's an understatement. Every night, he would come home and talk about his day, and I would listen—for hours. The weight I then carried around was unbearable, and I resented these "debriefing" sessions. I would gear up for when he would walk through the door, knowing I needed to be his support; I tried so hard to let him get it all out. After all, that was healthy, right? We don't want anyone bottling things in. The problem was that we were going over the same things every single night.

I went to have coffee one day with an older, wiser friend, and I shared with her that I needed strength. I asked her to pray for me.

She looked me square in the eye and said, "Honey, you got to put a stop to that. You are not his unloader; Jesus is. Besides, it doesn't sound like he is helping himself either."

She was absolutely right. It wasn't about being available to listen during a hard season. It was about moving on when you can't do anything about it. I went home and calmly and firmly said that was it. We would each get ten minutes to vent, and after that, we would enjoy ourselves and focus on the positive. I was not being insensitive; I was not shutting him down in his hurt, but I told him there comes a time when, after you grieve, you just have to move on.

Some people are complaining masterminds. They are the people who, no matter how great thing are, can find what went wrong. My husband is *not* one of these individuals, and odds are, if you have picked up this book, you aren't either.

There are times, however, when life can make you a complainer. For a short season, you become a downer. All you see is gray and more gray, and even your relationship can be colored that way. My trigger is days and days of rain. I love water—the sea, a lake, a pond, and even a little creek gives me such refreshing calm, but I truly believe blackened skies are a curse. Rain puts me in a mood. When it rains a lot, I start praying for so much sun that I actually want a drought, and Steve has to give me the ten-minute timer.

Life can give us enormous blows, but we don't get to write our stories; God does that. When I get down, it is because I am discouraged in what I cannot see as good. I can't see where God is going with the plot or even see the full story he is writing. I can get so focused on what I don't have, or don't want, or can't instantly make better that everything sinks.

We do have a choice. We get to choose how we live the story God gives us. My question to you today is this: are you thinking the best about your spouse? Are you giving your spouse the benefit of your best thoughts toward him or her? Are you communicating and being life-giving? Do you have a gut-level honesty with your significant other that no one else gets? Do you speak to each other as if you are desperately, madly, over the moon for each other? Are you watering your fern?

Instead of complaining, focus on what you like—and do more of that! If you love date night, go out more. If you love hot bubble baths with your spouse, go get in! If you love trivia or soccer, find a team. If you like his smile, find ways to make him smile more. If you like those jeans on her figure, buy her another pair. If you like comedy shows or wine tasting, go and laugh, sip wine, and do more of what you like. Stop complaining about what your spouse is not doing and thank God for what *he* is doing in you. Stop wishing she would do X, Y, and Z (whatever that is), and be grateful you get to do life with her.

If complaining and focusing on what you don't have is killing your relationship and your romance, what can transform it? Statistically speaking, much of relationship counseling doesn't work, the reason being that when you go to a counselor, you will unpack everything that is wrong. That can be depressing! Stop focusing on everything that is wrong, and start seeing what is right.

Jesus said, "Out of his heart will flow rivers of living water." We hope you drink more living water. We hope you see the gift God has given you in your marriage.

Steve says,

We have a list of tips for instant transformation, and we follow them on a regular basis. We stand firm on these things. These four tips can transform your relationship immediately to a better place. They can keep your fern growing and thriving. We do these things to give our relationship energy, joy, and connection:

Date

Go on a date. We are amazed at the number of couples who forget or have no idea how to date their spouses well. What does that look like? It's all about creativity and putting a little forethought into it. So often as time goes on, date night becomes either nonexistent or the same old, same old. Spice it up with a cooking class, mountain biking, drive-in movie, art gallery, sporting event, or concert. The definition of insanity is doing the same thing over and over again expecting different results.

If money is tight, or the babysitter cancels, we have become notorious for home dates. We put the kids to bed a little early and carve out time for us to invest in each other. We treat this differently than the average night (sometimes we even dress up). This idea has everything to do with igniting your romance for each other.

Place

Pick the destination where you want to go next, and talk about it. This is not a vacation where you visit family or bring the kids along. This has to be just the two of you. Anticipation is half the fun. Dreaming and planning this getaway can bring unbelievable joy to your relationship. It is kind of like when you were waiting to have sex—all you could think about was when you would get to do it and how much fun it would be once you finally did.

What do you want to see, experience, and accomplish on that vacation? This has everything to do with being in and on an adventure as a team. This thought is why many of us get married in the first place. We want to have someone with us and for us during the adventures in life. In modern culture and society, many of us do our day-to-day activities apart. Work, work trips, and the juggling act of kid activities can have you both running your adventures as individuals and not as a team. It can be disheartening. Going on a vacation together will help remind you what doing things together as a team feels like.

Position

Try to get out of the rut and have fun. In general, most people don't dream enough as a team when it comes to their sex lives. So often, these desires are kept quiet, and then the frustrations come out on the golf course with buddies or at the nail salon with the girls. I am shocked when I hear a person venting about his or her sexual desires but then find out that the person hasn't talked about it to his or her significant other.

This is not the time to focus on what desires are not being met but rather a brainstorming time, as a unit, to express what you want. It is super fun. This focus point has everything to do with your connection and intimacy. Remember the sexy jar mentioned in chapter 5? This is where you implement this.

Goal

Don't pick thirty-seven goals, and don't pick a personal goal. Pick one goal as a *couple* that you will work toward. Do you want to pay off your mortgage early? Do you want to start a company together? Do you want to run a marathon together? Pick one thing that you can do. This has everything to do with your purpose as a team. It is all about reminding yourselves that two are better than one (Ecclesiastes 2).

Chapter Questions

- What events have happened in your relationships that have shaped how you interact together?
- What is killing your proverbial love fern? What are three immediate solutions you can implement to nourish your relationship?
- What is a date, place, positon, and goal you want to do together?
- What do you like doing, and how can you do them more?
- How is complaining and pessimism affecting your relationship?

CHAPTER 9

Finding Naomi

—*Kate*

True love does not only encompass the things that make you
feel good, it also holds you to a standard of accountability.

—Monica Johnson

I am someone who if I say I will do something, I do it. So when I tell
you I will show up, I will. To add to that, Steve is a super-hard worker
and a very dedicated and loyal individual. We can't wait to continue our
journey together. We are full of life, energy, and vitality. We show up as
participants to our relationship. So how are you showing up for yours?

We want to go at our relationship as if we were headed for spring
break—bright-eyed, adrenaline-rushed, and pumped up. We want you
to think about your romance like that. We want you to show up every
single day of your relationship—to be fully engaged; to be so energized
about your relationship that people look at you and bet money you have
had nine cups of coffee and a chocolate doughnut.

Life is what you choose to make it; so is your relationship. You have
to be intentional and hold yourself accountable. I encourage you to go

for a higher level, and be inspiring. You have to be fully present and fully available for what you are about to engage in. That is how we run our marriage. We are all in, all the time.

Forget about Maintaining, and Start Cultivating and Creating

At what point do you start looking for inspiration in your relationship? Is it when your enthusiasm is waning, and you are lost? Is it when exhaustion replaces passion? Is it when fear trumps confidence?

A vital place to start the conversation on showing up correctly for your marriage is talking about cultivating enthusiasm. When you are excited about something, it's not work. Although it may be tiring at times, you love it, and you breath it, and you can't get enough of it. I have seen people who give ninety hours to their workweeks and not even flinch. Most of us shy away from such long hours. So why do some people enjoy it? They enjoy what they do so much that the hours and the work doesn't feel like work at all. We want you to stay in this space when viewing your relationship. Your passion for each other surpasses the "work".

To show up correctly, you must also have those people around you who will hold you to higher standards and to greater achievement than you may see yourself doing. Ruth is one of the best examples in the Old Testament to showcase this.

The book of Ruth tells of a woman who really messes up. Naomi strips her family away from their country and their people. I thought this was unique, as I knew a little bit about the exclusive nature of the Jewish culture. So I did a Bible study on it. I found out that Naomi and her husband moved because of famine in the land. She was frightened for survival. She sacrificed and lost. She tried to protect her kids, but she failed.

Have you ever done something out of fear? This is Naomi's story. In doing this, both her sons married far from home and to people not from their religious backgrounds. This was considered taboo in that day and age. Both her sons and her husband were buried in foreign soil. Despite this tragedy, Naomi became a legend for her daughters-in-law.

We do desperate things when we are starving. Whether it is spiritual, emotional, relational, or physical starvation, starvation brings out desperation. Are you in a place where you need to do desperate things?

Why is Naomi even mentioned in the greatest book of all time? The story is a tragic one for sure. The thing is, Naomi made such an impact in her daughters-in-law's lives that these women wanted to be with her. They wanted to follow her back to a land where they would be considered outcasts and lower citizens. They decided that they would leave their own home, friends, and families and head back with Naomi, in order to keep her in their lives.

Do you have anyone in your life who inspires such greatness that you couldn't even be paid to walk away? Naomi was this for her daughter-in-law, Ruth. Ruth wouldn't be caught without Naomi's influence in her life. This odd mentor figure brings out greatness in Ruth. Because of Naomi, Ruth was able to find the one man in the entire city who would value her in her new hometown. A man named Boaz would marry Ruth.

Why would this traditional, prominent man, lower himself to this relationship? Here is where the story gets interesting. Boaz was Rehab's son—the son of a foreigner. Boaz was part of another story with another famous non-Jew woman. Rehab, Boaz's mother, was a prostitute who saved her family by letting down a red cord out her window for some Israelite spies. She saved these men from near death. In return they saved her family from destruction when the city was overthrown. Boaz was probably the only one in the entire city who understood Ruth's "outsider" situation so completely.

This story is not only one of my favorites, but it also is the epicenter of true romance and heroism. To top it all off, Ruth is stated in the genealogy of Christ!

Salmon the father of Boaz, whose mother was Rahab,
Boaz the father of Obed, whose mother was Ruth.
(Matthew 1:5)

Where would Ruth have been if she hadn't had her mentor? Naomi coached Ruth on how to approach Boaz and how to do certain things in the culture. Without Naomi, Ruth's life would not have been what it was. Who are the people who instill excellence in a bountiful way in your own life? If you don't have this, find someone ASAP. Find someone who can cultivate greatness in your marriage.

We look up to some people because they are awesome at parenting and have incredible kids. Others, we look up to because they represent exemplary status in career growth and personal development. Some individuals are beautiful examples of a life focused on service and spiritual growth. Our most prized mentors are the ones who have rock-star–status marriages and push us to have that for ourselves. The individuals who radiate joy, fun, love, and growth will be the most incredible mentors you can give yourself. Marriage mentors are the best mentors. They can speak life into you when you don't see it yourself.

Without counsel plans fail, but with many advisers they succeed.

—Proverbs 15:22

You don't have to worry about getting it all right now, but you are accountable to God, and I hope that lights a fire under you. I hope it encourages you to be incredible in your marriage. I am not trying to create fear in you but to inspire deep motivation for what you have. Being accountable to God in your relationship means you have an active role in it.

I've mentioned how comfortable I was after we bought our first home and had our two miracle children, but when God calls you to something greater, you move. We didn't have all the answers, and we certainly felt like it was a big risk. Kind of like when Jesus asked his disciples to get back in the boat at midday and go fishing, after they had been fishing all night. I always wonder what they thought. They did it because … well, it was Jesus, and you don't mess around with anyone who changes water into wine. As expert fishermen and as tired as these men were, I am sure that there were a few rolled eyes and deep sighs at Jesus's request.

We were "fishing in the middle of the day" when we were to move away from our ten-year home base. Our friends were there. Our church was there. Our kids' preschool and our little neighborhood was there. The location was great and growing. Yet with all of our friends watching, we jumped into the boat, rowed out to the middle of the sea, and dropped our nets. We had no clue what would unfold, if anything, but we obeyed. We moved across town.

There will be times when you walk on water and times when you need to jump ship. Sometimes you will let down your nets, and they will break from being so full. God didn't call you into this beautiful romantic story to stay in the storm and in the boat. He calls you to walk on water! In your relationship, you are called to go big—to not shrink or apologize. Jesus was always calling his disciples and his people to big things. Don't look back over your shoulder and at the edges of the boat; leap into the vast ocean of the greatest adventure of this earthly life.

How in the world do we keep from sinking? By fixing our eyes on God. Most of us would say it drives us crazy when we are talking to someone, and that person does not look at us or pay attention. It makes perfect sense—just like when I look at my son and say, "Look at my eyes. Where are your eyes?"

I want my son to look at me and to see me. I also want him to see what he is capable of. When you look at your mentor, and he or she is speaking life to you, you know you can do anything. When my son is looking at me I know he is listening to what I am saying and that he is fully present and fully engaged. Our God wants us to fix our gazes toward him.

God wants our full attention so that we truly see him. He also wants us to see what we are capable of and that we are fully paying attention to what he has for our marriages. He is our ultimate mentor when it comes to our romantic relationships.

The Bible tells a story about a large storm. Jesus was there personally. The boat was battered because the wind was against it. Do you feel the wind is against you right now? In the story, Jesus encourages his friends to take heart and to not fear. Despite their exhaustion and timidity, he calls for greatness. He persuades Peter to get out of the boat and walk on water. Jesus tells his friend that all he has to do is maintain eye contact with him.

Let us encourage you to do the same. All you have to do is step out of the boat, just like Peter did. You get to participate in this amazing, miraculous journey that Jesus has set before you. Marriage is the opportunity to live out the very best of loving one another. Be brave and maintain eye contact.

We have this hope as an anchor for the soul, firm and secure.

—Hebrews 6:19

God is strong enough to anchor your entire marriage—through any storm, through any midday fishing trip, and most especially as you jump ship and walk on water. God is love. To know him is to know love. Your marriage is not only one of the greatest gifts from God to you but to your family and your friends as well.

Standing secure in God allows us to be courageous in our love lives. Our romantic relationships have the potential to shape a great future. Average is no longer acceptable. "Good enough" doesn't cut it in our marriages. We are called to go beyond the average in our love lives. We are called to greatness and excellence—to create an exceptional romance.

⁓

Chapter Questions

- We do desperate things when we are starving, whether that is spiritual, emotional, relational, or physical starvation. Are you starving in any areas right now and what are they?
- Who are two couples who do life as a team really well?
- Who are the people who instill excellence in a bountiful way in your own life?
- Who can you meet with this week to ask that person to be your Naomi?
- God didn't call you into this beautiful romantic story to stay on the shore and in the boat. How are you cultivating your faith to get out of the boat?
- How can you give God and your spouse better eye contact?

EXPECTATION LISTS

We thought long and hard about putting this at the back of the book. In one respect, it is extremely embarrassing, and we wish we could edit some of these early, horribly (and politically) incorrect thought processes. In another respect, it is amazing how many of them are still relevant and part of our core values to this day. We were asked to do this exercise in the months leading up to our marriage by our pre-married mentors. While there are many competing arguments around bringing expectations into your relationship (we agree with many of these points), this was a great exercise to see where each person was coming from and what was important to each party. Take it for what it is, and maybe you'll get a few laughs as well.

Steve's Expectations for Himself

- Be the spiritual leader of our house.
- Take the initiative to make sure we are involved in a church or actively looking.
- Create an environment in our home where Jesus Christ is glorified in all we do.
- Help out with cooking as much as I can.
- Take the initiative to wash the dishes every night so Kate can rest.
- Take out the trash.
- Help pick up around the house; keep it as clean as possible.

- Help out with cleaning the apartment or house.
- Be in charge of writing the bills and keeping track of our financials.
- Remember that work stops when I come home.
- Be sensitive to Kate's needs and desires.
- Reassure Kate that she is my number one.
- Spend some nights reading together.
- Continue some sort of Bible study that we do together outside of our own studies.
- Take Kate on dates, and be creative with them.
- Make sure we never lose our communication.
- Filter my decisions based on what God's plan is and how it will affect Kate.
- Pray for Kate constantly.
- Try to integrate her and my family into our vacations and holidays (sometimes).
- Keep family communications open, and try to pursue a relationship.
- Meet all Kate's sexual needs.
- Continue to romance her and pursue her heart, long into our marriage.

Steve's Expectations for Kate

- Take charge in cooking our meals. (Dinner is really important to me.)
- Allow me to help in cleaning up after dinner—my way of saying thanks.
- Take the lead in household things such as:
  o cooking,
  o laundry,
  o cleaning,
  o sorting through mail.

- Follow my decisions as head of our household.
- Trust me with my job; know that you will always be more important.
- Comfort me when I need it.
- Remember that words of encouragement are always welcome.
- Although I want your input, let me be in charge of our finances and spending.
- Meet all my sexual desires and needs.
- Be at home when I come back from work (as much as possible).
- Continue in your relationship with Jesus Christ; you encourage me so much.
- Find an outlet to use the talents God has given you.
- Be an at-home mom, once we have kids.
- Once our kids are in school, continue trying to teach dance.
- As a couple, find a church that fulfills both our hearts' desires.
- Pray for me so that I can hear from the Lord.
- Remain calm in arguments/disagreements.
- In everything, trust and love me.

Kate's Expectations for Herself

- Continue to grow and learn from the Word of God and my prayer times, inspiring Steve through my own actions.
- Prepare meals—breakfast, lunch, and dinner.
- Do Steve's laundry, including ironing and matching socks.
- Clean the house, including organizing, picking up after Steve (when he doesn't have time to do it himself), bringing in the mail, doing the dishes, and anything else regarding household pickup.
- Budget according to Steve's expectations with our money.
- Submit to Steve's authority, and give him honor.
- Go to Steve's business affairs that I must attend with him, with great respect and in proper attire.

- Play hostess to those Steve brings home for visits and dinners.
- Greet Steve every day with a genuine smile when he gets home from work, even if my day has not been the greatest (and give him proper space before unloading him with the troubles of my day).
- Pray for Steve continually.
- Help with financial stuff (in early marriage life) as I work my job diligently.
- Raise our children alongside Steve with proper love, care, and discipline (later on in our married life).
- Keep myself healthy and appealing for my husband.
- Continue to cultivate my girlfriend relationships, which I know are important for accountability.
- Continue to seek advice and encouragement from other married couples.
- Fulfill Steve's sexual needs and desires.
- Remember Steve's family's birthdays, and send cards.
- Continue the special relationship with Steve's mother.
- Give Steve the love and respect he needs, paying particular attention to his love languages.
- Help with washing cars, weeding flower beds, trimming bushes, and cleaning out the garage or attic.
- Reflect the character of God in my everyday living as best as possible (Ephesians 5:21).

Kate's Expectations for Steve

- Be the spiritual leader of our household.
- Pay the bills and balance the checkbook.
- Take out the trash.
- Mow the yard, and keep the cars washed, as needed.
- Make the proper time to share and continue romancing.

- Continue to seek advice and encouragement from other married couples.
- Love me as Christ loved the church.
- Pray for me continually.
- Cultivate your "guy time" with your buddies in a godly and proper fashion, with fun and accountability.
- Respect my father.
- Be sensitive to my needs as best as you can be. (I understand you won't always understand me.)
- Take the time to serve my love-language needs.
- Be the leader in how we raise our children.
- Remember our anniversary, my birthday, and (when they come) our children's birthdays.
- Fulfill my sexual needs.
- Communicate with me about what is going on in your life at work and your spiritual walk so I can continue to pray for you (specifically).

CONVERSATION STARTERS

- What's one instrument you would love to play but never have?
- What's your favorite holiday?
- Sunrises or sunsets?
- Beach or mountains?
- If you had a day all to yourself, with no obligations, what would you do?
- What chore do you despise the most?
- If you had a boat or private yacht, what would you name it?
- If you could redo your college major, what would it be?
- What friend do you miss the most?
- What was the best family trip while you were growing up?
- What's your greatest fear?
- If you could ask God one thing, what would it be?
- If you could take one year of your life to serve your community or world, what organization would you serve?
- What's a crazy vacation you want to take, and why?
- Where do you want to go on our next getaway—just us?
- If you could be proficient at anything by tomorrow, what would you choose?

Kate's Top Three Tips

1. Put down the phone.

I love my phone and what it can do now. It is a mini-computer, and social media is way fun! However, it is a real killer of conversations with my hubby, so I am very conscious of having phone-free zones. Our bedroom is one of those zones. We also have a no-phone policy at the table, and that includes restaurants.

2. Have more sex.

The average amount of sex for couples is two to three times a week. Some may feel that is a lot, while for others, it's not nearly what it should be. I don't want to have an average romance, so I am going to have a larger number than the average. Simple, right? Just get sideways in the sheets a lot more often.

3. Stay vulnerable and available.

We live in a world of filters and instant availability to everything. With this opportunity comes the struggle to hide behind an image and to not be authentic. To close ourselves off from the most important person in our lives by being busy and by being surface-level is one of the most detrimental things we can do. Choosing to be available is choosing love. Choosing openness is choosing intimacy.

Steve's Top Three Tips

1. Talk less; listen more.

Kate's and my willingness to truly listen to each other is one of the key determining factors in our marriage success. I cannot overstate the importance of communication. If this is working correctly, then everything else is a lot easier. The more you and I talk, the more we are inclined to escalate and dominate. Try to listen without getting defensive, thinking of your response, or being distracted by other things.

2. Give—it's bigger than you.

I love our world, but we are an extremely selfish society. It is very easy to get caught up in this mentality and not uncommon to spend an entire paycheck before it even hits your bank account. You have to be purposeful with your time and money; otherwise, culture will dictate where it is spent. Giving is all about getting eyes off you and focusing on someone or something else. It is both refreshing and healing. You will find new purpose and joy by stepping up to the plate here. Being generous is contagious!

3. Grace.

Humans are amazing creations. Our capacity, reasoning, logic, and physical and mental abilities, combined with our ability to love, makes us truly unique. We are far from perfect, though. This is especially evident in a relationship in which two unique individuals are blended together. We all fall short, and do so often. I'll be the first to raise my hand on this one. Grace is perfectly modeled in the character of Jesus. We cannot earn his love or do anything to deserve it more. In the same way, give grace despite these known shortcomings, if your spouse is truly making an effort to become a better version of himself or herself. Giving it freely to your partner is an amazing act of intimacy and love.

Date Ideas

- Share a late breakfast over mimosas.
- Take a long, quiet walk.
- Read a good book aloud together.
- Do a unique activity—cooking class, white-water rafting, building a fire pit.
- Gaze into a fire.
- Go to a rooftop bar.
- Ride roller coasters all day at a theme park together.
- Spend time in a hot tub.
- Cook a multicourse meal.
- Stargaze late at night.
- Watch the sunrise or sunset.
- Swing in a hammock.
- Go hiking.
- Eat a different ethnic food—our favorite is a Moroccan restaurant where you sit on pillows and watch fire dancers.
- Have a pizza picnic night—lay a blanket on the floor while you watch a movie.
- Have a game night.
- Try indoor sky diving (iFly).
- Try indoor rock climbing.
- Take a helicopter ride.
- Visit a dance club.
- Go to a concert or show.
- Attend sporting events, just the two of you.
- Train for a race as a team.
- Go to a gun range.
- Have a couples massage.
- Go kayaking.
- Take a camping trip.
- Get pedicures.

- Ride horses.
- Go ice skating.
- Go to an art-and-wine show.
- Attend wine and beer tastings.
- Go to a drive-in movie.
- Try apple, blueberry, or pumpkin picking.
- Rent scooters or Vespas.
- Have a scavenger hunt.
- Rent a limo.
- Drive around to look at Christmas lights, with coffee.
- Visit a dueling piano bar.
- Take ballroom dance lessons.

ACKNOWLEDGMENTS

We would like to give a very big shout-out to all the people who have helped us in this journey of writing. The process of learning, growing, and doing this has been incredible, and we could not have done half of it without the help of the following talented and incredibly dedicated individuals:

Mom and Dad Rockwell, who were Kate's first editors as a homeschooled kid, decided to help us out by once again pulling out the red pens. They continually gave feedback through this entire process. This has been invaluable and has meant the world to us. We can't thank you enough.

Jim Bowes, you are one of the few people outside of family who has witnessed our entire relationship as a couple. We are so grateful for your influence and wisdom. You and your family are a true picture of Christ and his love.

Boyd Bailey, you took Steve under your wing instantly and provided so much wisdom and guidance as we tried to chart a course for this writing/ publishing journey. Your counsel was spot-on, and you cheered us on the entire way. You and your wife are a gift and breath of fresh air. Thanks for your continued support for the generations behind you.

Frank Bell, you have been a crucial role model since before we were even engaged. Thanks for pushing us to walk out this vision, even when fear and doubt seemed to take center stage. Your wisdom as an entrepreneur, CEO, father, husband, and fellow Christian has played a crucial role in our success as a couple.

Ted Lowe, we are so grateful that God brought you into our lives. Thank you for your openness and your candid and transparent perspective on marriage ministry, as well as providing a platform for us to grow and expand. Your friendship is life-giving, and we appreciate all you've done for us in these early stages.

Alea Moore Photography and meadowlark1939.com—the go-to for wedding and lifestyle photos! Alea helped us create beautiful backdrops and images for our website and book design. We admire and treasure her grace and calming nature in the professional world, as well as in our friendship. She is a highly sought-after photographer and has been featured in multiple blogs and magazines. She and her husband have built a farmhouse, have four daughters, and hold a venue for wedding and romantic getaways of all kinds. She is truly enchanting!

Jared and Megan Fulks are the next generation of marriages and a dynamite couple! Their help with social media platforms and web designs were irreplaceable. They believed in us when this concept was just a thought, and their support has been motivational and inspiring. They are remarkable in every way. We love you!

99designs.com—we cannot emphasize enough how incredible this company is. So many individuals helped and collaborated with us for our cover design, and they made it so much fun. The professional atmosphere and focus on detail were top-notch. We highly recommend this company to anyone who needs a logo or design of any kind.

Lulu.com—thank you to the entire team for providing an unmatched service for helping to give brand-new authors and writers the chance to make a dream a reality. You've made this journey epic. So many people came together to take a draft and turn it into an exceptional product. You will always have our recommendation.

ABOUT THE AUTHORS

Kate Dahlin is a former ballet teacher and health instructor, now working as a full-time home manager, blogger, and personal lifestyle coach. Her goal is to help instill the life skills that individuals need to have a more fulfilling and well-rounded vision of what's possible.

Kate has danced her way across America, run a half marathon, done multiple mission trips, dealt with infertility, and transitioned to home life after a career in the arts. She loves to read a good book, walk on the beach, cook, and empower women for exceptional living.

Steve Dahlin is an articulate and methodical technology sales representative who has worked for the last twelve years with some of the largest tech giants in the industry. As a people-person through and through, he will never shy away from starting a conversation with a complete stranger.

He is an avid drummer and artist, makes killer pizzas on the grill, and minored in Bible. Steve loves to travel with his wife, take his kids on dates, and play golf when he has time. He was a state finalist in swimming, ran a half marathon, hiked several Colorado 13ers (peaks between 13,000 and 13,999 feet in elevation), and had a spot in the Ben Affleck film *The Accountant*. He has been blogging for several years and enjoys working with individuals on how to create balance in life, while fueling positive momentum in their relationships.

Kate and Steve call the greater Atlanta area their home, and they dream of one day living in a beach house. They have two children and a golden retriever and love to spend their weekends working in the yard and sipping wine. They work with pre-married and married couples on an ongoing basis and have been affiliated with Northpoint Ministries for the last nine years. Their passion for seeing Millennials and Generation Z thrive has them working on concepts and ideas to facilitate greatness for these generations.

You can connect with Steve and Kate by following them on their social media platforms and blog, and by checking out their website.

Facebook: @stephennkate, @katemdahlin
www.facebook.com/stephennkate.dahlin
Blog: www.katemdahlin.com
Website: www.anexceptionalromance.com

APPENDIX

Application Exercises

- Buy a journal. Take time to invest in this.
- Write in it the date and what number journal this is for you.
- Then write out your favorite Bible verse in the front pages in your own words. Take time to ask God to make this verse your own and your mantra for this season you are walking through right now.
- Now write out the sacred vow from chapter 8 as your own.
- Write the vision statement for your relationship.

Questions to Answer in Your Journal

- What kind of energy and focus will you give your relationship with God?
- Do you want to work on the most important relationship you have on earth? If you do, why have you not focused on it?
- How do you cultivate it personally? What is your action plan?
- Are you dedicated to take the time it will take to love your spouse?

Kate's Personal Verse (Psalm 37:3–7a, paraphrased for my own life)

3. Trust in Me, and do good Kate; Dwell in the land, and eat on My faithfulness.
4. Delight in Me, My dear child, Kathleen. And I shall give you the desires of your very soul.
5. Commit your way to Me; Trust in Me Your Lord, for Kate, I am worthy of it! I shall bring it to pass.
6. I shall bring forth your righteousness as the light, And your justice as the noonday.
7. Rest in my arms, and wait patiently for Me.

Steve's Personal Verse

Even the youths grow tired and weary, and young men stumble and fall; but those who hope in the Lord will renew their strength. They will soar on wings like eagles; they will run and not grow weary, they will walk and not be faint. (Isaiah 40:30–31)

Our Verses as a Couple

Guard the good deposit that was entrusted to you--guard it with the help of the Holy Spirit who lives in us. (2 Timothy 1:14)

And the LORD answered me: "Write the vision; make it plain on tablets, so he may run who reads it." (Habakkuk 2:2)

In chapter 9, we talked about killing the love fern and that we could make a list of all the things we have seen that have broken and sabotaged a marriage, keeping it from exceptional status. So without further ado, here is the list:

Connection Killers

• Money

Steve and I aspire to many things, but one at the top is managing our money wisely. We want to get this right. We want to look back, decades from now, and see the rewards that resulted from prudent and consistent investment.

Tensions can rise quickly. Money is one of the leading reasons why couples seek counseling, and it is no wonder. Money is not just about debt ratios and risky versus nonrisky individuals. I'm talking about what drives people, what the end goal is, how satisfying work is (or if it isn't), and how things change and evolve with time and kids.

Here are our personal tips for diving into the topic of money:

1. Don't go into debt. Your mortgage should be the *only* exception. We believe in this, even for school debts.
2. Give and serve.
3. Live off one income. If both people are earners, a best practice is to use only one income and save the other.
4. Save for travel, and go big.
5. Share your banking, credit cards, bills, and investments—no exceptions!
6. Always choose a work/rest balance. I use "work/rest balance" rather than "work/life balance" because some work is home-based, but that doesn't mean that those who work from home have a balance. The phrase *work/life balance* means either that work isn't a part of life, which is completely false, or that home life isn't work. Anyone who

has raised children or has been a home manager knows differently. Choose a life that creates both rest and work for both parties, and enjoy both to the fullest.

- Not going to bed together
This is so important. We have said this before, but it deserves another touch point. Not connecting at night with your spouse can cause your marriage to unravel as time progresses. It becomes much more dangerous territory than the kids sleeping in your bed or someone now sleeping in a basement bedroom. It becomes a chasm between the two of you that is hard to recover from.

- Screen time (Chapter 2)

- Not doing date night

- Secret accounts, passwords, or media

- Public insults

- Excess

I [Kate] believe in moderation in almost all things. Too much sleep—you're lazy. Too much sugar—you're a glutton. Too much exercise—you're obsessed. Too much of extended family—you lose relationships (or secretly wish you could have "too much drink"). Too much of the holiday hoopla—you end up turning into the Grinch.

First of all, break down the problem into chunks. Maybe you are drinking every day or bingeing on the weekends. Or maybe it's a loved one you need to raise the flag with. It's not an issue yet, but if not addressed, it will become one. This could be anything. It could be too much shopping, too much phone time, too much work, too many projects, too much sugar, too much TV, too much take-out, or too much obsessing over being thin.

This issue is creating a rub. It is not how you want to run your home, so you choose to get in front of it. You no longer will ignore this or scoot around it. You have decided you will create exceptional in every area, and that means this topic too. This is not going to hold you back.

The solution we have for this is simple: pick a number. When it comes a to a lot of things in life, we set numbers or a time slot for ourselves. The Bible talks about gaining wisdom from this.

Teach us to number our days, that we may gain a heart of wisdom.

—Psalms 90:12

Many of us do this without even knowing it—one-hour meetings, five days for work, rest on Sunday. Six weeks of school, one week off. Every two weeks we pay the bills. Every season shift, we deep-clean the house and change the air filters.

When it comes to exercise, I try to work out more than half the week. Seven days in a week means three times doesn't cut it for me. To exercise four times a week is fabulous, but seven times is obsessive. So for logical reasoning, we do a very similar idea with our drinking habits.

For us, this system means we make continuous and calculated steps to implement every day. We are numbering our days and tasks, and putting in place our plan of execution. The Bible says we are growing wiser by doing this.

If one oversteps the bounds of moderation, the
greatest pleasures cease to please.

—Epictetus

- Not dressing for success

We have noticed that once people get married, there tends to be a decline in fashion for their partners. Some of this is good. It means you are comfortable.

However, the statement about dressing for success at work is true for your marriage too. We have a dear friend who changed his entire wardrobe after about five years into their relationship, and all of a sudden, she had the hots for him in a totally different way. I am not saying to buy an entirely different wardrobe, and I am not encouraging fast fashion, but if your partner only sees the weekend sweatpants, are you truly showing up for your marriage? Are you showing up more for work than you are for your romance?

We know a couple that we love to mimic in this. They are both entrepreneurs and work from home, but oh my, do they know how to turn heads and to step up their game when they need to. They don't do it just for work but for each other. They are beautiful and fun on the hiking trail in their T-shirts with holes, but on date night, they can make everyone wish they aged like they have. No insta-filters needed!

- Lack of praying

Here are shocking statistics: while 50 percent of first marriages end in divorce, and 78 percent of second marriages end in divorce, less than 1 percent of couples who pray together daily end their marriages. These are stats from a study done by Christopher Ellison at the University of Texas in 2010. We encourage all couples to look it up. We have personally seen the proof in this. Both sets of our parents pray together. Prayer benefits every aspect of life, and our relationship was no exception.

We are happy to report both sets of our parents are still joyfully married and deeply in love. Praying not just *for* your spouse but *with* your spouse creates intimacy and unity. The lack of it could be your downfall.